Magazines for Children

A Guide for Parents, Teachers, and Librarians
second edition

Selma K. Richardson

American Library Association
Chicago and London 1991

Cover and text designed by Charles Bozett

Composed by Alexander Typesetting Inc.,
  Indianapolis, on a Datalogics typesetting
  system in Century Schoolbook

Printed on 50-pound Lynx Opaque, a pH-neutral
  stock, and bound in 10 point Carolina cover stock
  by Imperial Printing Company

The paper used in this publication meets the minimum requirements
of American National Standard for Information Sciences—Permanence
of Paper for Printed Library Materials, ANSI Z39.48-1984. ♾

Cover Credits
Chickadee and OWL logos © The Young Naturalist Foundation 1990
Reprinted with permission
Cricket logo reprinted by permission of CRICKET Magazine
Faces and *Cobblestone* logos reprinted with permission of
Cobblestone Publishing, Inc.
Ranger Rick® logo used by permission of the National
Wildlife Federation
Art from *Stone Soup* reproduced with permission of the
publisher, the Children's Art Foundation
Zillions logo reprinted with permission of the publisher,
Consumers Union of United States, Inc.

Library of Congress Cataloging-in-Publication Data

Richardson, Selma K.
   Magazines for children : a guide for parents, teachers, and
librarians / by Selma K. Richardson. — 2nd ed.
      p.   cm.
   Includes index.
   ISBN 0-8389-0552-8 (alk. paper)
   1. Children's periodicals, American.   I. Title.
PN4878.R5   1990
051' .083—dc20   90-45152

Printed in the United States of America.

95 94 93 92 91   5 4 3 2 1

Contents

Appendixes

Subject Index   137

Preface

The first edition of *Magazines for Children* was reviewed widely and favorably. It was received enthusiastically by many school and public librarians who found the book a useful and valuable tool in selecting and acquiring magazines and in answering reference and readers' advisory questions about the quality and content of children's magazines. The descriptive and evaluative annotations of some 90 magazines were written to help meet the needs of librarians serving children and the needs of teachers, parents, and other adults seeking information about the variety of magazines published for children. The first edition's focused list, taking from *Periodicals for School Media Programs* those titles meant for children, allowed not only a separate grouping but also the opportunity to provide lengthier annotations. Descriptions could be more thorough in *Magazines for Children* and provide details inappropriate to the earlier *Periodicals for School Media Programs*. It was hoped that the intended audience would find a separate and unique publication helpful. And, apparently, librarians, teachers, and parents did.

Magazines, however, come and go. Some titles in the previous edition of *Magazines for Children* have ceased publication. (Some titles have even come and gone in the hiatus between the two editions of this work.) The time has come, if not already past, when a new edition is of the greatest necessity. Titles that continue to be published need to be reassessed to determine whether or not they have sustained their focus and quality and to note any changes in content and format. Therefore, all titles listed in the earlier edition were reevaluated and annotations revised accordingly. Each annotation was reconsidered in view of recent issues of the magazine and an updated editorial profile, when it was available. The descriptive and evaluative phrases of the earlier annotations that remain as true and pertinent today as they were in 1982 are left intact, although there is little that is unaltered. Much new material is provided in the annotations of the titles that were listed in the previous edition. Numerous new titles were also considered, many entering the market since the earlier edition. These titles were assessed to determine whether or not they met the selection criteria for this book. Those that did have been entered into the body of this work. Annotations for them were written in keeping with the descriptive and evaluative commentary of the first edition's annotations. Special efforts were made to find titles published by and for ethnic groups, although this search was not as fruitful as would be desirable. Magazines from religious publishing houses are now included in an appendix. It is hoped that the call for such information will be met by this listing. Needless to say, this new edition is coming out none too soon.

No publication comparable to *Magazines for Children* exists. The catalogs of magazine jobbers do not evaluate and seldom annotate the publications listed. Children's magazines are noted in comprehensive sources about periodicals; however, frequently it is only bibliographic information that is given, with the exception of the costly *Magazines for Libraries* and *Magazines for School Libraries* (Bowker, 1989 and 1987), in which a paragraph for each of the children's magazines selected may be found. Lists appear now and then in newspapers, professional journals, magazines for parents, and works about children's books and reading. These lists, nevertheless, are usually prepared for specific purposes and, therefore, carry a limited number of titles with annotations that are at the most but a few sentences. Neither do two recent titles supplant or take away from the uniqueness of this book. *Magazines for Children* (Donald R. Stoll, editor; copublished by the Educational Press Association of America and the International Reading Association) provides a 30-page directory listing along with a brief annotation for each title. *Using Children's Magazines* (Nancy E. Seminoff, Perfection Form Co.) concentrates on ways to use magazines in classroom instruction and limits descriptions of magazines to brief commentary on about 30 titles.

Magazines bring valuable information and pleasurable experiences to children. These publications can expand the worlds of childhood, opening avenues of exploration in ways other media cannot; they are, in addition, able to satisfy ever so many current interests, both common and unusual. The subscription price proves to be a sound investment when a child and a first-rate magazine are so suitably matched that the child looks forward to the magazine's regular arrival. Even in times of economic restraint, few libraries would consider eliminating the magazine collection, although selection policies might be refined. Few schools would remove the option that allows children to purchase classroom magazines. And homes, while adjusting priorities and weighing the value of toys, amusements, sports equipment, and food treats, would only with great reluctance sever the bond between child and subscription. Magazines are essential in homes, schools, and libraries.

Magazines for Children is meant to be of assistance to people who want to know about the magazines reviewed in this book. Descriptions and evaluations are intended to allow teachers, librarians, parents, and other interested adults to make judgments about certain titles for purchase, whether for child, classroom, or library. Teachers not only need to know what magazines support curriculum subjects and other activities, but they should be aware of the titles available for classroom orders. Yet all too often, when a classroom order is gathered, students may not be given the opportunity to choose among publications despite our society's emphasis on choice and the fact that the classroom would be enriched by a mix of different and competing magazines.

Librarians must carefully and judiciously shape subscription lists because magazines form an integral part of the materials and services provided for children in school and public libraries, whether the goals specify curricular, informational, or leisure intents. Parents and other adults seeking to link the interests and abilities of a child with a personal subscription sometimes know of the few magazines that have high visibility because of large or long circulation records and vigorous promotional campaigns; however, there are many other fine magazines. This book has been planned to alert adults to the selection available and to highlight especially for their exceptional qualities a few magazines that might not be so well known. Upper-grade elementary and junior high students themselves might find answers to their questions about magazines listed in this book, which includes periodicals primarily published for children through age 14 (or eighth grade), and available by single and classroom subscription; at newsstands; and through memberships.

Acknowledgments

This edition has roots in the earlier edition in several ways, a few of which need to be mentioned here. Certainly the consultants who suggested children's magazines and reviewed my list must be given credit for identifying and confirming many of the titles included. Their advice was most helpful in shaping the first edition, and many of their ideas continue to be found in this edition.

The librarians and reviewers who encouraged my efforts to gain acceptance for a separate work about children's magazines should not be forgotten at this time. Some of these same people were supportive of my stance regarding the need for a new edition. The arrival of a new edition is an occasion for all of us to rejoice and a confirmation of earlier aspirations.

The many librarians who have passed along words of appreciation for the first edition need to be acknowledged on two counts. First of all, it is rewarding to be told that one's work is valued. Secondly, praise goads one on, and I felt compelled to be as exacting with this edition as possible. On both counts memories of hours of drudgery are quickly dispelled by a few kind words.

Many of the publishers of children's magazines were exceedingly cooperative in providing sample issues and the information needed about their publications. My requests were frequently acknowledged with letters that opened doors to their publishing firms and made it very easy for me to seek further assistance when needed. Telephone conversations often, in addition to providing specific information, gave me needed boosts and encouragement through expressions of appreciation (and empathy) for the work I was undertaking. The cooperation of ever so many publishers lightened my load considerably and made for several joyful days.

The dispatch with which some publishers responded to my requests was also very much valued.

Although there is a certain injustice to naming some, and not all, publishers that were, indeed, very helpful to me, I do wish to recognize some. Among the publishers represented in this book by entries for their companies because they publish three or more magazine titles, my special thanks are extended to Rhetta Aleong, Editorial Assistant (*3-2-1 Contact*), Children's Television Workshop; Katy Dobbs, Editorial Director, Welsh Publishing Group, Inc.; Elizabeth A. Rinck, Editor, Children's Better Health Institute; Laura Ruekberg, Executive Editor, Curriculum Innovations Group, General Learning Corp.; Irwin Siegelman, Editorial Director, Field Publications; and Carolyn P. Yoder, Editor-in-Chief, Cobblestone Publishing Co. Other editors and staff members who were particularly helpful, to name another half dozen, include Charlotte Baecher, Editor, *Penny Power*; Marianne Carus, Editor-in-Chief, *Cricket*; Sheila Cowing, Editor-in-Chief, *Shoe Tree*; Christine Lord, Assistant to the Editor, *Merlyn's Pen*; Nancy Mack, Editor, *Odyssey*; and Claire Miller, Managing Editor, *Ranger Rick*.

Words of acknowledgment and appreciation are due those publishers that so willingly and quickly furnished sample issues and information even though their publications did not turn out to be listed in this book. The reasons for exclusion were often related to scope, not the quality of their magazines. Many of the publishers of religious materials promptly sent samples from the range of their publications. They were particularly understanding as I tried to sort out reasons for inclusion and exclusion, which could not be articulated early in the process. Their mailings enabled me to assemble and view the various types of publications and to make decisions about the kind that would be most usefully listed in this book. This groundwork should also facilitate any further investigations in this area.

Mary Nelson, graduate assistant, with patience and persistence, worked on seeking out and organizing the materials from the religious publishing houses. Additionally, she was both helpful and cheerful about tackling the many details a book such as this requires. She handled graciously a great deal of the telephoning that was necessary. My thanks go to her for being such a fine working partner.

Sally Eakin of the secretarial staff of the Graduate School of Library and Information Science has an indisputable record for furnishing me with supplies the moment I express a need for them. She also handled ably the mailings this project necessitated. All her willing efforts are appreciated, now as ever.

And, last but not least, one could not in the most utopian of circumstances want for a secretary more talented and able than Kathy Painter. With the greatest dispatch, she transforms my scribblings into copy that, then, doesn't seem so awful to me after all. Her incredible skills at the keyboard are transcended only by her desire to satisfy. If she were ever to exact her price, I would have to go to debtor's prison. I am most appreciative of her contributions to this book.

Introduction

Purpose

The purpose of this book is to provide a guide to magazines published primarily for children. For librarians serving the needs of children, the book is meant to be a source of the information that is important in evaluating magazines, valuable in selecting and acquiring them, and helpful in answering reference questions about the nature of certain titles. For teachers, this is a handbook that identifies and describes magazines that can be used in classrooms to support the curriculum and for other needs and activities. For parents and other adults, the book is designed to be an aid to becoming acquainted with the availability and quality of children's magazines so that adults can make informed choices about subscriptions or gifts.

The magazines for which annotations have been written are intended by their publishers for children through 14 years of age and for students in grades through the eighth, whether in an elementary, middle, or junior high school. (Of course, some of these publications are also meant for young people above the specified age and grade spans.) The titles included accommodate a range of interests and reading abilities. The subjects or emphases of the magazines are varied, although a few might be designated "general interest." The magazines that have been selected for review can be used with curricular subjects or read during leisure hours and have the potential to be informative and entertaining, whether the user is a browser, a neophyte at research, or an industrious innocent depleting the contents by following instructions to draw, cut, and fold. Some magazines are available at newsstands and by subscription; however, many may be purchased only by subscription, and a few must be obtained by means of membership. Subscriptions for these magazines can be ordered by individuals, classrooms, and school and public libraries. Some publishers gear their advertisements to specific audiences and also have different prices for different subscribers, but all the magazines selected for this edition are available for subscription by individuals and libraries.

Librarians

Librarians, school and public, need to develop magazine collections that are in keeping with the selection policies of their libraries. Drawing upon users' requests and suggestions and capitalizing on a knowledge of magazines, the librarian creates and shapes a subscription list that is responsive to the expressed and unexpressed needs of the library's community, taking into account the pressing constraints. This is not a passive task; the competent librarian alerts the people served—children, their parents, teachers, and others—to new magazines and titles unknown to them and seeks to involve these users in evaluating and selecting magazines for the collection.

Astute judgments cannot be made without sufficient information. Magazines are constantly making modifications in their intent and format, not to mention their frequency of publication, and it is difficult for anyone to keep up with all the changes. This book is designed to bring to the librarian descriptions and evaluations of magazines currently published for children and to help the librarian gather information about the availability of titles and the quality of their format and content. With this information and an understanding of the community to be served, wise decisions can be made that will result in a magazine collection fashioned to meet the needs of users.

Teachers

Teachers, those who are employed in regular classrooms and those who work with special children or special subjects, need to know of magazines that can be used as tools of instruction. Magazines can enrich the study of science, math, social studies, and the language arts; some provide offerings in music, art, foreign languages, and physical education; and some stimulate inquiry into such multidisciplinary subjects as consumerism and the environment. Teaching and learning strategies often incorporate practice and activities with magazines. Many classrooms order current events publications designed to develop and exercise skills related to certain subjects and to strengthen the habits of newspaper reading. Students are sometimes urged to use magazines to find information and gather material for reports.

The experiences magazines can provide relevant to reading and visual discrimination are seemingly boundless. Whether to extend or reinforce information, to prod students to go beyond or dig deeper, as assortment of magazines centering on a number of subjects is available to quicken the interests of children. Much of the material in magazines is packaged in ways that make reading (or looking) altogether pleasurable. At once magazines are informative and entertaining, amusing and instructive. In some instances, no other medium can capture children's interests or expand their worlds as effectively as magazines.

Magazines as a medium are a fascinating communication tool and could well become the subject of a classroom or library unit that investigates the extent of the field, methods of production and marketing, unique characteristics and conventions of this form of publishing, and criteria for evaluating titles. Teachers making subscriptions available through classroom orders can and should consider all the titles published that might be appropriate to the children in their classes. If choices are offered to children, they can be alerted to some of the factors that should enter their decision making, in itself a valuable experience with magazines. This book is intended to provide teachers with information about the variety of magazines published for children in a readily accessible framework that enables teachers to draw descriptions and evaluations as needed.

Parents

Parents and other adults at times seek information about children's magazines that can be purchased for the home. Browsing in libraries and at newsstands may yield some suggestions; however, neither location ever carries all the magazines published primarily for children. Many parents want their children to have the satisfying experiences subscriptions can bring. Children sometimes beg for subscriptions and, when the wish is granted, almost always look forward to the regular arrival of issues. Magazines can open new avenues of exploration for children, providing the means by which they are able to travel near and far. Certain titles may encourage new interests or nourish already acquired interests. Some may broaden the outlooks of young readers, while still others allow for greater specialization.

As a means of communication, the magazine is noteworthy for its regularity and currency, even when updating such "ancient" subjects as history and archaeology. The magazine is a medium well suited to relaying recent developments swiftly and one with which children should be familiar. Parents, grandparents, aunts, uncles, friends, and other adults who want to give children presents that will be delivered over the course of a year should consider what delightful gifts subscriptions can make; many adults are even likely to be amazed at the quality of the product for the price. But how do adults learn of the magazines available in order to select the ones most appropriate for the child or children in mind? This book lists many of the available options and sufficiently describes the magazines so that choices may be narrowed to those publications most appropriate for a given child. Additionally, physicians, dentists, psychologists, and other professionals who stock their waiting rooms with magazines for children might well consider the titles listed rather than relying solely on the suggestions of advertisements or salespersons.

For librarians, teachers, parents, and others, over 100 children's magazines are described and evaluated in this book. *Magazines for Children* is meant to be a guide for those who want to bring together children and magazines and who, to do so, want to know about the titles available and about their quality and characteristics in order to make informed decisions.

Criteria

The first criterion a magazine needed to meet for inclusion in this book is related to intended audience. The publisher had to indicate that the magazine is meant for children under 14 years of age or for students in grade eight and under. Several classroom periodicals are designed for grades seven and up. These magazines have been considered because at least part of their audience falls within the range stipulated and because such periodicals can be and are used by children in grades lower than the eighth. Titles intended for grade eight and up have not been included.

The second criterion concerns quality. This book is not meant to be a highly selected source; however, the magazines chosen are generally accepted as being appropriate for children. While some titles are barely satisfactory, others are exceptional. Nevertheless, it was thought that descriptions and evaluations of the lesser ones would be as important as those for the very best magazines to parents, teachers, and librarians, who are quite likely to come across the titles. Each magazine probably would be of some benefit and interest to at least some children. All are worthy of consideration in developing magazine collections in school and public libraries, in guiding selection and offering options to children in classrooms, and in choosing subscriptions for the home. A few magazines might bring objections from individuals, but it is hoped that to a certain extent the informational needs and recreational pursuits of children under 14 will be served by the titles making up this compilation.

In describing and evaluating the magazines, content and format were examined. These were not easily separated; content pertains to subject, and format to how matter is conveyed. One concerns what is said, the other how material is assembled and presented. Content was considered acceptable when it was in keeping with the interests and capabilities of children. Format was deemed appropriate when the packaging was consistent with the magazine's focus and likely to appeal to the intended audience.

With regard to content, the magazines were studied to determine whether the subject matter of each was of concern and interest to children and, when a more specifically delineated audience was identified by the magazine's publisher, whether the material was appropriate for the selected target group. The types of features making up a magazine's content were noted. Typically, stories, articles, and games and activities, as well as other amusements and challenges that are the stock of children's magazines, fill the pages of these publications. Thus, a magazine's content had to be suitable for the intended audience, whether this included all children or only a particular group. The subject focus and special interests of magazines are often stipulated by publishers within the magazines and in advertisements. Additional statements were frequently enclosed in correspondence to the compiler. The distinguishing characteristics specified, which have been quoted in some annotations, were pitted against content of the issues examined. If particular bents pervaded publications, editors ought to have acknowledged them. When controversial issues were addressed, authors ought to have suggested, at the very least, that differing viewpoints exist. In addition to the acceptability of the contents for children, observations were made about the consonance of the magazine's subjects with the prevailing preoccupations of children.

In considering text, both fiction and nonfiction had to be presented with a sense of accuracy and truthfulness. The qualifications of the writers were noted, when furnished, and their abilities were judged by their products. Styles of writing within a magazine needed to be compatible and meet a minimal level of acceptability, although no attempt was made, either with fiction or factual writing, to seek a specific style. The writing had to be readable, cast in a manner that easily moved the reader forward. Most desired was language that was vivid and engaging; vocabulary had, at least, to be interesting. When writers presented their thoughts lucidly or handled ably the constraints of controlled vocabulary, their efforts were praised. Various tones and points of view were allowable; however, condescension was so labeled. In nonfiction, it was expected that the treatment be clear and direct, the material organized and comprehensible. Because children are frequently urged in magazines to make or do things, instructions for such projects had to be clear, simple, and accurate. Not only was material in an article to be arranged logically, but a logic needed to either be evident or quietly underlie the presentation of the content of an issue.

In studying the illustrations, attention was paid to the type of illustrative material presented. Photographs and drawings are used heavily in children's magazines; however, there are circumstances that call for graphs, charts, maps, and diagrams. The medium and subject of any illustration had to be appropriate to the magazine and, when applicable, to the magazine's special audience or subject. Authenticity and accuracy were utilized as standards, as was creativity when appropriate. If illustration was prime, as is true of many magazines for the very young, the work was assessed with regard to its quality, allowing for limitations of production, and the care exercised in selection. For all illustrations, however, judgments were made about the quality of reproduction. Sizes of illustrations were noted, especially when a different size would have been more suitable. Appraisal of decorative matter centered on whether it tended to enhance or detract. The illustrations were surveyed, not only as they stood on their own but with respect to their compatibility with text. Illustrations were not required to be subservient to text; a complementary relationship was the criterion, as was a balance or ratio appropriate to the particular magazine; and when a ratio was specified by the publisher, whether it had been adhered to was noted. Pictorial matter had to be pertinent to and extend and clarify the text if that was its purpose. Styles of illustration—a variety was considered admissible—had to be in harmony with the specific texts and with the issue as a whole. The use of color too was evaluated.

The cover is an important element of this particular medium. A magazine cover is a dependable, predictable feature, even when differing pictorial matter appears from issue to issue. The nameplate too is usually as distinctive as a signature. Therefore, covers were viewed to determine whether they reflected the magazine's content and truthfully announced it. It was expected that covers be attractive, inviting, unerring signals of the content. To the pictorial work on covers were applied the standards required for interior illustration.

Among other particulars of format considered was the magazine's typeface. Its style and size had to be suited to the audience and the scope of the magazine because the legibility of print affects readability. Distinctive and appropriate typefaces and unusually fine choices were commended. The type of paper and its quality were examined. Durability also was used as a standard but was tempered to take into account what is reasonably required of particular types of magazines and the medium itself. Newsprint was very acceptable for certain periodicals, while for those that carried features to punch out or use as board games, other specifications must have been met. Magazines that put substantial stock in color photography wisely elect to publish on glossy paper. The number and size of pages were reported, and when something was unusual about amount or dimension, this was commented upon. And last, but certainly not least, attention was given to elements of design, of the pages and package, to assess whether the total effect suggested a unity and the layout of pages helped sustain interest from cover to cover.

Exclusions

Magazines in some categories have been excluded from the annotated list. Although some of these excluded classifications, indicated below, are frequently represented in magazine collections of school and public libraries, such periodicals are beyond the scope of this book.

Magazines published primarily for adults, such as those of the spoof-and-satire and role-playing-games varieties, among many others

Magazines targeted for young adults age 15 and older, particularly in the categories of music, fan, fashion, and lifestyle (One such title even requested not to be included in a list of magazines for children.)

City and metropolitan magazines and newspapers for children (and sometimes also for their parents), their content and ads best serving local interests

Newsletters for children, although titles are beginning to appear about such diverse topics as young entrepreneurship and the plight of the economically disadvantaged children of the world

Magazines published for classroom use but unavailable as single subscriptions mailed to one address

Serial publications that lack the magazine characteristics of variety in contents and regular dating of issues, even though mailed as subscriptions

Serial publications that resemble workbook pages more than magazines

Professional journals for teachers, administrators, and librarians

Magazines for parents

Comic books

Appendix A contains titles of religious publishing houses.

Methodology

Obtaining Titles

For the first edition of *Magazines for Children*, consultants who were geographically spread across the United States and representative of school and public libraries were asked to furnish subscription lists and to suggest other titles. These consultants held positions in the spectrum that included an elementary school library media specialist, a supervisor of services in a large public library system, and a children's services coordinator for a state. Thus, as a group, the consultants exemplified many circumstances in which children's magazines are used.

Lists of children's magazines that have appeared in newspapers, magazines, and books about children's literature and reading were checked for titles. Comprehensive directories of periodicals were examined for sections listing magazines for children. Catalogs of jobbers were searched. Much browsing was done at newsstands and libraries for further suggestions. The possibilities were gathered and then sifted to eliminate those titles entirely out of scope.

Obtaining Magazines

To acquire magazines and information about them, letters were mailed to publishers requesting current data and statements about their magazines that would be helpful in describing and evaluating the publications. Each publisher was asked to complete a form regarding specific publication data and the readership of the magazine(s) and to furnish additional information or materials (brochures, scope statements, market studies, and so on) about the emphases and purposes of the magazine and its special qualities and features. Publishers were also asked to supply supplemental materials and guides available to subscribers. The publishers were requested to send three recent issues typical of a year's subscription, not special or enlarged issues. Publishers were most cooperative. All of the magazines annotated in this book have been studied.

Annotations

Following each title in the annotated list is the name of the publishing company if it differs from the magazine's title. When two addresses are reported, the first is for the editorial office, while the second is for subscriptions. If only one address is specified, all matters are handled at the same location. Frequency of publication is indicated, and specific times of publication are noted for the magazines that furnished this information unless listing the exceptions would become unwieldy. The cost of a regular annual subscription is given, as well as the price of other subscriptions, particularly those placed as multiple orders and mailed to one address.

The annotations attempt to describe and evaluate the magazines as thoroughly and carefully as possible, using the criteria outlined in the previous section. Every effort was made to provide annotations that would be helpful to potential subscribers to whom sample issues may not be readily available. The special subjects or emphases of the magazines are mentioned because these are important facets in linking publications with intended or target audiences. The contents are described with reference to the types of material carried, including that which is in text and illustration. How the contents are conveyed and packaged, the formats, are discussed with regard to tone or approach, elements of design, and matters related to printing.

The first paragraph of an annotation often carries a brief overview or general description of the magazine. Succeeding paragraphs provide specifics and greater detail about the observations made in the first paragraph. Frequently, an in-depth description of a particular issue is presented, along with evaluative commentary about the content and format. When a specific issue was chosen for close scrutiny, care was exercised in its selection to ensure that the sample was typical of other issues of the magazine. The overriding intent in delineating one issue is to impart information about the nature of the magazine and its content, not just the character of a single issue.

No attempt was made to make the annotations conform to a specific number of words. Annotations are of various lengths because they contain the information thought necessary to do justice to the publication for the purposes of this book. A few magazines are quite specific in content and need little explication. Other periodicals find the largest part of their audience in secondary schools, and therefore, the annotations refer primarily to the use of the magazines with children under age 14. A few annotations are lengthier than the average. Some evaluations probably betray the writer's desire to assume the role of critic who illumines and calls attention to worthy features that might go unnoticed. Certain of these magazines merit being placed in the hands of many more children, but their publishers' budgets and the channels for advertising are constricted. In all instances, the annotator was guided by the desire to describe and evaluate the magazines for parents, teachers, and librarians seeking information about the periodicals. For some magazines, descriptions are not readily available anywhere else, and in some circumstances, sample issues may be difficult to obtain.

The ages and grade levels reported are always those specified by the publishers. When the annotator disputes the extent or narrowness of the ranges suggested, the reasons are cited. Those who work daily with students are well aware of the range of reading abilities in a group of children of even the same chronological age. All users of this book are urged to consider age- and grade-level designations as rough estimates or general indicators of the reading difficulty of the magazines and, furthermore, are implored to allow children, when it comes to magazines, to have some say in finding their own levels of satisfying returns.

Within some annotations, reference is made to the availability of editions for teachers and to guides, newsletters, and other supplemental material prepared for parents and teachers. Some of these publications are free, while others must be purchased as special subscriptions. The reader seeking further and updated information about these special items is encouraged to write to the publishers. A thorough discussion of these publications for adults is out of scope for this book.

Some of the magazines are published in braille. A few magazines are recorded on audio discs. The availability of these editions is indicated in the annotations and in Appendix B. These special formats are available by subscription, through interlibrary loan, or from the National Library Service. Readers in need of further information about the availability of editions in braille and on disc should write for the free booklet entitled "Magazines in Special Media," which is available from the National Library Service for the Blind and Physically Handicapped, The Library of Congress, Washington, DC 20542.

If a magazine is indexed in *Children's Magazine Guide*, the title of that index is found immediately following the annotation.

Seven publishers included in this book prepare three or more magazines for children under age 14. For each of these firms, an additional entry is provided under the name of the company. Within the special annotation, there is a general description of the publisher's magazines and a list of the titles annotated in this book. The list is arranged according to the age or grade levels for which the magazines are intended, beginning with those for the youngest children. The list should be helpful in looking over the products of a certain company, particularly in seeing the relationship of one title to another, and can serve as a cross-reference to the annotations. The seven publishers are: Children's Better Health Institute, Children's Television Workshop, Cobblestone Publishing Company, Curriculum Innovations Group, Field Publications, Scholastic, and Welsh Publishing Corporation.

Timeliness

The descriptions of the magazines, the publication data, and the prices reported in this book are based on issues published in early 1990. Subscription costs can be expected to rise during the lifetime of this book because publishers budget to meet higher production and mailing costs and make adjustments for inflation. Nevertheless, because prices are likely to rise somewhat uniformly, it will be possible to continue to compare, at least roughly, the cost of subscriptions for a few years.

Undoubtedly some magazines will cease publication before this compilation is next revised (or even before this book is published), and some will make modifications in content and format. A book does not have the advantage of monthly issues; thus, it will not be possible to update changes until the next edition. It can also be expected that new magazines will appear and that some that have suspended publication will pick up again. Change, however, is a stable characteristic of the magazine industry, and this book must go to press.

How to Use This Publication

Arrangement

The annotated entries form the major section of this book. Magazines are presented alphabetically by title. Each entry provides publication data followed by a descriptive and evaluative annotation. If a publisher issues three or more of the magazines annotated in this book, an entry is also made under the name of the publisher and the publisher's magazines are again listed and briefly described. Cross-references also are furnished when magazines might be known by their subtitles or some other words.

Appendixes

Several appendixes have been placed in this book to extend its usefulness by providing further aid and information to librarians, teachers, and parents. Appendix A lists magazines of religious publishing houses. Publication data and targeted age levels are provided. The purpose and scope of the list are described in the appendix. Appendix B brings together all the references in the body of the book about editions for the visually impaired.

Appendix C classifies the magazines listed in this book according to the ages and grade levels suggested by the publishers for their magazines. Such groupings should facilitate locating titles for certain children. Necessarily, two lists are provided because some publishers target specific grade levels, while others identify ages. This particular appendix also allows for scanning the titles, which are annotated in the main section of the book, with regard to level of difficulty, but readers should keep in mind that age- and grade-level designations are approximations.

Two appendixes carry information that users of this book may deem helpful. If publishers furnished data regarding the year in which their magazines were first published, it is reported in Appendix D. Circulation statistics, when furnished by the publishers, are recorded in Appendix E.

Subject Index

A subject index at the end of the book groups the titles under about 20 headings. Because many of the subject headings are broad, the index should not be used for access to very specific or limited topics. However, each title in the main section of the list has been placed under a subject heading. Cross-references lead to subject headings used and to related subject headings.

The Collection of Children's Magazines

The librarian might well be the only person having the opportunity to alert children and adults, students and teachers, to all the magazines published for young people. The library might be the only place some people will be able to find out about the periodicals intended primarily for children, and particularly about those magazines of superior quality.

The peculiarities of distributing magazines are such that potential subscribers cannot find all the options assembled in one place. For certain titles, newsstands are the outlet; however, even reasonably well-stocked newsstands seldom carry more than a half dozen magazines especially for children. Other titles are available only by subscription; however, some magazines offered by home subscription have vigorous advertising campaigns (and little need of further promotion by libraries), while others must operate on a shoestring. Classroom magazines are published for children; however, it is usually the teacher who decides whether or not subscriptions will be entered and which title will be ordered. Although even the school or public library cannot be expected to house the full range of magazines especially prepared for children, the librarian (and library) can be committed to providing as many magazines as possible and to furnishing publication information and even sample copies of titles not in the collection.

Perhaps it would be helpful, first of all, to mention briefly the special characteristics of this print medium so important to a library's collection.

Most of this discussion first appeared in *Illinois Libraries*, January 1985.

Characteristics of Magazines

The magazine is generally considered a print medium that fully utilizes illustration and contains the written word. The picture-text blend is typical of most children's magazines. Children use magazines for entertainment and information, for assignments and leisure activities. Uses are not readily categorized; some tasks are pursued with pleasure. The motivation or need of the individual usually determines the approach to particular titles. Contents might be scanned or mined.

Books and magazines are similar in a number of ways; however, certain characteristics of magazines distinguish this medium from the one that fills most library shelves. These special characteristics are frequently the elements that attract browsers and devotees to magazines. The features are worth noting because they have bearing on the reasons for collecting and providing magazines in a library, and they need to be considered in evaluating and selecting titles. Besides, children can be alerted to the characteristics of the medium by the librarian, whether through informal or formal instruction. (For the very young, serial publication is a new concept.)

Magazines are published (or at least dated) at regular intervals. Publication schedules are meant to be fixed and dependable so that the arrival of issues can be readily predicted. Material in magazines is usually recent or timely, having some particular connection with the present or with prevailing interests. Even magazines that treat historical topics present features that are prompted by marking the date of some event.

The most significant characteristic of magazines, however, is that each one is prepared for a carefully defined target audience. Intended readers are usually described by age and/or level or type of interest in a subject. An age group, obviously, has been designated by publishers that intend their magazines primarily for children. Some of these publishers even specify quite limited age levels for their magazines. The focus of a magazine is sharpened by identifying particular subject interests. Certain magazines specialize in health, current events, or sports. Even for titles that cover wide-ranging topics, it is not difficult to picture an intended audience. (Consider *National Geographic World*, *Highlights*, *Wee Wisdom*, or *Sesame Street*.)

Magazines usually offer variety in their contents and in the ways they present the contents. Nevertheless, each issue forms a whole, and the various issues are related to one another by a focus.

Deviations are kept within a defined scope. It is this particular characteristic that clearly distinguishes a magazine from a book. The mixture of content and layout appropriate for a magazine would be considered a hodgepodge in a book. And yet in a magazine, the mixture is generally consistent from issue to issue. Subscribers expect the subject matter and format to remain fixed. Any changes need to be in keeping with the whole and viewed as improvements by a vast majority of the subscribers, who have paid in advance for the product.

Two notable features of magazines are the cover and the contributions from readers. The cover is the crucial link between the viewer and the content. The cover reflects the content and can be expected to be a clear and vivid representation of the general nature of the magazine and specific topics within its scope. Covers of a particular title also show consistency from issue to issue, even though each cover is usually different. A basic design is generally adhered to. Within the framework identified, variations are presented. The lettering of a magazine's title is as distinctive and unique as a personal signature. Any alteration would signal a personality change in the magazine. The nameplate is always clearly visible. Furthermore, every magazine is named with great care. Much thought, even research, goes into finding the word or two that will encapsulate the contents and entice the target audience.

Subscribers are urged to contribute to magazines in various ways, and their contributions are an important element of most periodicals. Among the submissions are letters, questions and answers, advice and opinion pieces, responses to surveys, and items that describe interests or hobbies. Among original works submitted are poems, short stories, articles, artwork, and a variety of puzzles.

Magazines can embrace a variety of writing styles and illustrations within any issue. Such diversity is not usually tolerated in a book. Illustrations within an issue might serve to decorate, explain, or enrich printed material and are frequently used to entice the reader. Within the subject scope, an issue's content might be presented in fiction stories and nonfiction articles, in short items and lengthy pieces. And with regularity, there is usually some form of game, craft, experiment, or activity for readers.

Purposes the Collection Serves

The magazine collection rightfully claims an important place among a library's offerings and serves several fundamental purposes. Obviously, a library purchases magazines so they will be used. While it is desirable for the magazine collection to be used heavily, it is unrealistic to expect that all magazines will be worn out equally. Nor should volume of use be the sole criterion for selection.

A collection can suggest the variety of magazines that is published. To suggest variety is also to acknowledge that different people will like (or dislike) different titles for different reasons. It seems fitting to encourage and preserve diversity in the collection. There can be variety in the types of magazines and in the treatment of subjects. Although the children's magazine field is not developed enough to have many magazines competing for a certain audience, there are, for example, enough science titles (and each quite different from the others) that choices can be offered in this area.

The library's collection can introduce to users titles that are not widely known, as well as titles that are meant for quite specific audiences. Some magazines have, and always will have, few subscribers. Other publications are targeted to readers with very particular interests. Through the collection, magazines worthy of promotion can be brought to the attention of children and adults. Unlike the magazines of high sales and broad interests, these titles often need word-of-mouth recommendations to survive. If the librarian can connect a reader of the intended audience with such a magazine, an important match has been made.

The magazine collection should include titles of unusually fine quality. (This is not to suggest that such magazines are the only titles to be ordered.) People generally expect a library to carry noteworthy materials and the librarian to be knowledgeable about the most highly regarded sources. Appropriately, the magazine holdings can satisfy the needs of children and adults seeking the best in this print medium.

The collection can serve to encourage personal subscriptions. Just as children are urged to develop their own libraries of books (through their use of the library collection), the magazine collection suggests titles that children might want to receive as personal subscriptions. And curiously it might be a terribly mutilated library copy that prompts youngsters to request their own subscriptions. A "used-up" magazine hints of a popular title. Moreover, some children will want to be assured that they will have the pleasure of cutting up, filling in, and punching out that personal subscriptions allow.

The library needs to suggest to users the array of children's magazines that is published. A substantial collection can do this visually. Children and adults can see in an attractive display of current issues the titles that are reasonably well known and the titles that are less familiar or intended for very specific audiences. Within the variety of magazines displayed, users should be able to find the few titles that are noteworthy for their quality.

Promoting the Collection

Several techniques might be employed to promote the use of the library magazine collection. Attention can be given to strategies for making the collection highly visible. Magazines can be incorporated into programs and services offered by libraries. But first, consider how important it is for the librarian to be aware of the contents of recently arrived issues if they are to be fully utilized.

Except for information that users find on their own, the librarian becomes the access point for matter in recent issues of magazines. No automated or printed indexes now available can keep up with the arrival of magazines in the library. Thus, it is necessary to file in the computer of the mind the contents of newly received issues so that the information can be retrieved when users ask questions that can be satisfied by a certain article or activity in a magazine. Contents must be known by the librarian in order to make the vital connections.

Visibility

Covers are built-in billboards for the contents of magazines. The area dedicated to housing current issues of magazines should allow for making readily visible the covers. Innumerable principles of advertising have gone into developing covers, and librarians need only let the covers be seen to capitalize on the marketing research. Most libraries do display magazines in a prominent location, and when protective covers are needed, transparent ones are selected.

Beyond the continuing display of current issues, special bulletin boards, showcases, or exhibits might be developed to highlight magazines. Librarians often supplement their supply of seasonal and holiday materials with issues from earlier years that carry pertinent stories and activities. For some children and adults, this assemblage might serve as an introduction to some titles they hadn't known.

A particular magazine title might be promoted by displaying back issues. Such an exhibit suggests the magazine's coverage over a period of time. The publishing history of a magazine can be conveyed by featuring the changes that have been made during its life. If certain magazines have been kept, some children might be curious to see the issues of the month and year they were born.

Magazines from the beginning of this century and even earlier sometimes become available to libraries. A display of these issues can point out similarities and differences between former magazines for children and those of today. Reader contributions, illustrations, fiction and fact, regular columns, humor, and amusements all can be found in the first magazines published for children. Additionally, such a display can help define the medium for children.

Bulletin boards, files, and notebooks can be designated as places for children to leave their comments about their favorite magazines, articles and stories they enjoyed, or parts of certain issues they particularly liked. Other displays or exhibits can feature things children have made or done that were suggested by magazines. The possibilities are numerous because many magazines seek to keep children busy or "doing." Prominence might be given to craft projects, science experiments, poems created, photographs shot, consumer investigations, and reports of excursions. And rather than fussing about destructed issues, buy extra copies and spotlight the things pages can be turned into.

Programs

The magazine collection can be promoted by using titles in the ongoing programs and activities that libraries offer to children and their parents and teachers.

As of late, there has been a significant interest in reading aloud in the home, somewhat encouraged by a number of recent books on the subject. Young children are dependent upon a reader to interpret the printed word for them. Several magazines for preschoolers, although highly pictorial, include instructions and ideas for further discussion in the small print meant for adults. When parents are seeking materials to share with their children, they can be reminded of the valuable matter in some magazines.

This sharing, however, need not be limited to very young children. The contents of magazines are such that they are easily slipped into conversations. (Adults are likely to refer to something they have read in a magazine or newspaper.) Therefore, even more so than books, magazines make a splendid vehicle for exchange of thoughts and comments between child and parent or other adult. The reading of fine magazines does not pose a tedious task for adults; in fact, they too will probably find the magazines informative and amusing. A real partnership (or a first-rate two-way conversation) can evolve from each person's interest in finding out what parts of an issue were savored or dismissed.

As with some books, certain magazines of superior quality will need to be introduced to youngsters by adults. *Cobblestone* comes to mind. Its intent to make American history fascinating can readily be appreciated by adults who have been subjected to dry textbooks. As parents, teachers, and librarians truly sample the diverse content of this magazine, it is not unlikely that they will feel compelled to share the title with someone in its target audience.

Some of the library programs prepared for various age groups can either center on magazines or in part introduce magazines. An animal story from a magazine might be told in a preschool story hour; an adventure tale might be highlighted for older children. The nonfiction material in certain magazines might be explored with a group of children. The activities and possibilities within the covers of even one issue might be plumbed. Special characteristics of the medium can be mentioned to young children and studied more thoroughly with older children. Reasons for indexing magazines can be discussed, and instructions in the use of *Children's Magazine Guide* (Bowker) can be given. Both children and adults can appreciate a librarian's lively talk about how to evaluate magazines. Children might review titles or issues for their peers, either orally or in writing.

Most of all, every opportunity should be grasped in planning programs to make users aware of the variety of magazines in the library's collection and to illumine the few that are of high quality.

Descriptive List of Magazines

Action see *Scholastic Action*

ALF *Magazine*
Welsh Publishing Group, Inc.
Edit: 300 Madison Ave., New York, NY 10017
Subs: P.O. Box 10559, Des Moines, IA 50340
Quarterly; $7.80

There can be no doubt about the leading character of this magazine started in 1989. His name is in the title; he is pictured on the covers and at the centerfolds. The fun-filled magazine parallels the television show "ALF" with its special brand of humor and peculiarities. About half the pages feature regularly appearing items. The other pages carry seasonal pieces—holidays and times of the year on earth and on Melmac, Alf's home planet. A few pages of ads promote products children would find of interest. Some ads are more readily distinguished from content than others. Full color is used throughout the 32 pages of each issue. The illustrations, mostly drawings, are peppy. The writing is snappy; fans will chuckle over the twists and asides. The quarterly is intended for children 8 to 12 years of age.

The titles listed on the contents page refer to presentations one or two pages in length. An exception is "The Melmatinee," the script of a three-act play of four pages that has transported the likes of Mary Poppins and William Shakespeare to the "regular TV-style English" and situations on Melmac. Among the captions appearing in every issue are "Gimme Four!", the editor's introduction to the issue, and "Letters from Earthlings" from readers to ALF. "Be There or Be Square" updates the latest fads and fashions ("coolest things") and unearths curious facts. "What's Cooking at Cat-Sup Diner with Stella" describes gimmicks with food and recipes along with the advice, when necessary, "grab a grown-up to help you." Unusual questions from readers receive strange answers in "Ask ALF," who often reflects his lifestyle in the responses. In "Big Yuks!" are printed a half dozen "thigh-slapping, side-splitting, gut-busting jokes." The amusements of other pages offer word puzzles, board games, instructions about drawing, and things to cut out or color.

Art & Man
Scholastic Inc.
Edit: 730 Broadway, New York, NY 10003
Subs: 2931 E. McCarty St., P.O. Box 3710, Jefferson City, MO 65102
6 issues during school year: September/October, November, December/January, February, March, and April/May
$11.50; $5.95 each for 10 or more subscriptions to same address

Prepared under the direction of the National Gallery of Art, this 16-page classroom periodical is meant for junior and senior high students, but the content of the beautiful, glossy-coated pages can be appreciated by those on both sides of the intended range. A thematic approach is used in each issue to show the relationships between art and cultures and the forces that fashion artistic expression. Within a recent school year, four issues focused on major artists—Gauguin (discussed below), Caraveggio, Imogen Cunningham, and David Hockney. The other issues centered on artists of ancient Egypt and American impressionists. On every 8-by-10⅞-inch page and the cover are reproduced in exquisite full color the paintings and other works of art that are the subject of the articles and special sections.

The subject of a recent issue is "Gauguin: Working with Color." As the title suggests, the theme allows for a study of the life and work of Gauguin and a consideration of color. The three articles at the front, each two pages in length, discuss Gauguin's use of color to express emotion and innermost thoughts, while the four regular sections of the second half of the issue tell how other artists have followed in his footsteps and how students themselves can work with color. The centerfold, "Masterpiece of the Month," is a reproduction of *The Siesta* by Gauguin.

In this particular issue, the first article, "The Savage from Peru," gives an overview of Gauguin's life with special emphasis on his early years as a painter. His time in Brittany and the development of his style while in the region are treated in "Images of the Spirit." The third article, "Search for Paradise," draws attention to Gauguin's move to the South Pacific and his paintings of Tahitian women. Each article is accompanied by full-color reproductions of his paintings. "Art Spotlight" in this issue introduces 20th-century artists who discovered new ways of working with color. In "Artist of the Month," a medalist in the Scholastic Art contest offers a self-portrait, in interview and acrylic. "*Art & Man* Workshop" provides guidance in creating with color, particularly how to express emotions in color. The back page, "Arts Alive," briefly notes two contemporary American artists who create quite different effects with their use of color. The theme, as usual, has been carried out exceedingly well. The mix of text and illustration is near perfection. Much can be learned and absorbed from the informative and handsome pages.

Although targeted for grades 7 through 12, this splendid magazine could, and should, be introduced to children in upper elementary grades who can be guided to an interest in art. There is no comparable publication. The quality of the content and format makes the magazine appropriate for all ages in search of an engaging introduction to the world of art. Families that enjoy going to museums will undoubtedly want subscriptions. But perhaps more importantly, museums of the world and private collections are both brought to subscribers. And the pages are not simply filled with paintings; the eminently readable text reveals information about the works and their creators.

The magazine's edition for teachers is sent free with 10 or more classroom subscriptions. As an individual subscription, it costs $20.50 and does include a copy of the student's magazine. For homes and libraries, the edition for teachers should be ordered. Four uncut pages (8 by 10⅞ inches) provide background material about the issue and specific articles and sections, as well as a bibliography of books and audiovisual materials. The pages, when opened out, provide on the verso a poster. In the issue discussed above, the poster is a reproduction of the painting of the centerfold.

Barbie
Welsh Publishing Group, Inc.
Edit: 300 Madison Ave., New York, NY 10017
Subs: P.O. Box 10798, Des Moines, IA 50340
Quarterly; $7.80

The subtitle reads "The Magazine for Girls," and one might add particularly the girls interested in clothes, hairstyles, and Barbie dolls. Barbie, in her ever-changing wardrobe, greets readers from the cover. The contents page announces seven or more items under "Features" and four or more regularly appearing columns under "In Every Issue." Among the features, however, are two pieces that are consistently published: "The Barbie Poster" of the centerfold and "The Barbie Story," a three-page excursion sure to delight the intended audience. (In one issue examined, the story centers on Jazzie, Barbie's teen cousin.) The contents page conveys the flavor of the magazine with a full-color photograph of a young (female) professional model in stylish apparel. About 10 pages of ads generally reflect the interests of the intended audience in clothes, toys, popular books, movies, and foods including cereals. The 32-page, full-color quarterly is meant for girls 6 to 12 years of age and has been published since 1984.

Among the regularly appearing columns are "Love from Barbie," another picture of the doll and a greeting for the season, and "Your Page," letters from the devoted readers and occasionally artwork. "Let's Talk" is an advice column answering questions sent in. "What's Happening" highlights the world of entertainment with announcements of new audio and video recordings, movies, and books, as well as television programs and other hot items. "Tricks & Teasers," on the last numbered page, offers a colorful word puzzle or two. The features usually center on fashions for girls; the full-color photographs showcase enchanting models. One article often describes how to create a special hairstyle. Another feature is the interview; issues examined spotlighted teen television stars, an author of a popular series, and a Barbie model. Usually one article in an issue ranges more widely; among topics discussed have been photography as a hobby and visiting a museum.

Bonjour

Scholastic Inc.

Edit: 730 Broadway, New York, NY 10003

Subs: 2931 E. McCarty St., P.O. Box 3710, Jefferson City, MO 65102

6 issues during school year: September/October, November, December/January, February, March, and April/May

$9.50; $4.95 each for 10 or more subscriptions to same address

Intended primarily for students enrolled in first-year French classes, this 12-page monthly carries picture stories and features to aid in developing facility with the language. A French-English vocabulary list, arranged in the order of the appearance of the French word in the issue, should help the beginner over troublesome passages. Other clues are found in the pictorial matter, which is plentiful and mostly in color. Next to each page number is the French word for the numeral. The magazine is just about the same size (7¾ by 10¾ inches) as other Scholastic periodicals and is published on newsprint.

In recent issues, the center pages feature Carnaval and food and dining preferences of the French. Regularly appearing pages are "Cher Bonjour," letters from readers here and abroad; fashions in "La Mode"; and television programs and stars in "La Télé." Entertainment personalities usually make appearances in the issues' text and photographs. A cartoon, "Hoxy et Gégène," puts to practice vocabulary skills and tests comprehension. Recipes require an understanding of French in addition to kitchen lingo. The back cover of four rectangles is meant to be cut up; on one side of "Les Fiches" is a photograph or drawing, and on the other is brief text about the picture, which is usually about some news item or current interest. The full-color front cover is often quite attractive, even alluring.

The edition for teachers is available for $20 but is free with over 10 subscriptions to the student magazine. Classroom teachers, of course, would want to have this edition for the teaching suggestions and the additional activities. If the magazine is purchased for the home (not its intended audience although a possible one), the edition for teachers does include a copy of the student's magazine.

Ça va is the French magazine for the intermediate level, and *Chez nous* is prepared for the advanced level.

Boys' Life

Boy Scouts of America

1325 Walnut Hill Lane, P.O. Box 152079, Irving, TX 75015

Monthly; $13.20

Published primarily for Boy Scouts, this monthly presents articles about and activities for outdoor life, sports, and recreation. The exhilarating cover illustrations announce the active interests promoted within. About a half dozen informative and well-written articles and a fiction story make up the middle third of the magazine. Numerous short pieces, about a page in length, precede and follow the center portion. Many of these are columns and comics that appear regularly. Projects and activities are proposed in abundance. Full color is used in the pictorial matter of most of the major articles, as well as the ads. The magazine is intended for boys 8 to 18; however, boys can't claim sole possession of the interests covered in the magazine's 70 pages.

The format of the contents page was made more lively with the 1990 issues; however, the categories used to arrange the contents remain the same. On the top half of the page are listed the "Articles" and the "Fiction" story. The specific titles are printed in boldface, and under each is a sentence to entice the reader. On the page's bottom half are four columns, each with an illustration. The column on the left usually announces the issue's special feature. The other columns, altogether listing about two dozen short pieces, are captioned "Comics," "Columns," and "For Scouts and Cub Scouts."

The nonfiction articles serve a range of interests. Each issue contains one article about a Scout activity such as mountain climbing, canoeing, or bike touring. All articles are highly pictorial, usually with full-color illustrations. Some writers are members of the editorial staff; others are experts in the fields of the topics or are free-lance writers. The major articles in one issue treat the following subjects: a Scout camping trip in California, sports video games, the expedition to find the Titanic, a professional football player, and an early submarine. In another issue, the cover story highlights the adventures awaiting those who visit the Scout wilderness bases. Other articles in the same issue introduce in text and illustration dolphins, raccoons, famous Eagle Scouts (now men), and the work of the animation studios of Walt Disney. A feature to appear four times a year is launched in the same issue—the "Bank Street (College) Classic Tales." The travels of Gulliver are condensed to a 16-page comic strip. Don Quixote and Marco Polo will follow.

The fiction might be a story full of adventure, a mystery, a humorous tale, or light science fiction. The protagonists, if not all the characters, are boys. Donald Sobol and Gary Paulsen are among the well-known authors published in the magazine. Other tales are apparently by free-lancers or lesser-known writers.

The entries under "Special Features" provide directions for making things (a desk set, bird feeder, or key chain) and doing things (collecting paper route money, growing sprouts, or making models). Regularly appearing "Columns" include "Hitchin' Rack," letters about the magazine from subscribers (including requests for features that just happen to appear in the issue at hand); "Hobby Hows," answers to readers' questions; "Scouting Around," news and notes about Scouts and Scouting events; and "Think & Grin," jokes sent in by boys (and a girl or two). Other regular columns cover science, nature, the outdoors, ecology, history, magic, health, bicycling, stamps, coins, and books. The new format has given a larger typeface to the captions of these columns.

Under the "Comics" category, five color comic strips appear rather regularly. In the Scout family, the youngest cartoon characters are the "Tracy Twins," followed by "Pee Wee Harris," while the older and more serious Boy Scouts pursue their activities in "The Pedro Patrol." "Scouts in Action" tells true stories of notable deeds of Scout members. "Bible Stories," not boxed but usually a half-page illustration, often shares the page with the "Tracy Twins." A recent addition to the comics is "Norby," a mixed-up robot created by Janet and Isaac Asimov. Other comics are listed on the contents page under "For Scouts and Cub Scouts" and include "Dink and Duff" and "Webelos Woody." "Tiger Cubs" presents a full-page puzzle in color and a monthly riddle.

The format of the magazine continues to be attractive, with many illustrations, often in color, printed on glossy paper. Color photographs are clear and well chosen. Artwork for major articles is striking and frequently covers a full page or a double-page spread. The 8-by-10⅞-inch monthly necessarily packs in the features that would appeal to the 10-year age span of its intended audience; however, the overall impression is not one of haphazard packaging. Recent renovations constitute minor improvements toward sprightfulness but no major reallocations or refurbishing other than on the contents page.

The purpose of *Boys' Life* is to promote "the program and values of the Boy Scouts of America: physical fitness, citizenship training and character building." To this end, the articles and columns offer material to help the Scouts learn the skills necessary to advance in the program. The subtitle "The Magazine for All Boys" makes note of the broader reaches of the periodical. There is very little about the participation of girls and women in sports, adventures, or the world at large. The monthly will find its avid readers among the Boy Scouts.

An edition is made available in braille by the Library of Congress.

Children's Magazine Guide

Calliope
Cobblestone Publishing, Inc.
30 Grove St., Peterborough, NH 03458
5 issues a year
$17.95

Formerly *Classical Calliope*, this magazine has gone through several transformations during its first decade. Beginning in September 1990, the name change will bring a shift in emphasis and a move toward being more like the other fine magazines, *Cobblestone* and *Faces*, from this publisher. The subtitle, "World History for Young People," explains in part the expansion of coverage beyond the ancient world (especially the Greek and Roman civilizations), which was the subject of *Classical Calliope*. World history, meaning West and East, will be explored through the Renaissance.

As with the other magazines of Cobblestone Publishing, each *Calliope* issue will center on a theme. The record of the other titles is unsurpassed among children's magazines with regard to the remarkable development of a theme from a variety of perspectives. An understanding of the subject evolves from various types of articles and illustrations and the accompanying activities and puzzles. Five issues are to appear in a year. Each will be 7 by 9 inches in size and bring 48 pages from the annals of world history. The first sentence in the guidelines for writers reveals the prime consideration of the publisher. The editor seeks "historical accuracy" in all submissions and lively and original approaches to the subjects.

Theme issues for the first year in new dress promise to be quite impressive. In lieu of being able to review an actual issue, the five themes and some of their subtopics are mentioned here: "Great Explorers to the East"—Alexander the Great, the Egyptians, the Portuguese, and Marco Polo; "From Byzantium to Constantinople to Istanbul"; "Epic Heroes"—Gilgamesh, Odysseus, Siegfried, and the *Mahabarata*; "Major Naval Battles"—Ramses III and the Sea Peoples, Salamis, Lepanto, Actium, and the Vikings; "Lost Cities"—Knossos, Machu Picchu, Great Zimbabwe, Mohenjo-Daro, and Persepolis. The prospectus is, indeed, auspicious.   *Children's Magazine Guide*

Career World
Field Publications
> Edit: Curriculum Innovations Group, 60 Revere Dr., Northbrook, IL 60062
> Subs: 4343 Equity Dr., Columbus, OH 43228
> Monthly during school year: September–May (9 issues)
> $15.95; $6.25 each for 15 or more subscriptions to same address

"The Continuing Guide to Jobs and Your Future" (the subtitle of this classroom periodical) should be very valuable to senior high students, although the publication is intended for grades six and up. In junior high and elementary schools, where the world of work is explored, some of the articles will provide good background material and current information. The articles that introduce jobs and professions are likely to be of more interest to younger readers than the how-to articles about seeking employment.

Each issue carries as its first article a major one with a special focus. The coverage in a year is, indeed, broad and certainly a strength of the magazine. Even the lead articles suggest many types of jobs within an area, whether the focus is on engineering, serving the elderly, becoming an entrepreneur, or driving vehicles. The features explore careers from several angles, thus conveying to young people information not only about specific jobs but also the settings in which these jobs are pursued. Among regular captions on the contents pages are "The Voc-Ed Connection," "Getting Hired," and "New Ways to Work." "Zeroing In" and "Profile '90" discuss specific jobs and often feature individuals successfully employed. Among the regular departments are "Jobs for Students," "TNT" (trends, news, technology), "The Lighter Side of Worklife," and "Your Turn," which answers subscribers' questions about education, jobs, and careers. The "Offbeat Job" is without fail a curious one.

The writing is clear and informative in this 32-page monthly. The typeface is legible, and text is given organization by subheadings and other forms of dividing. Black-and-white photographs are the most frequently used type of illustration. Charts, diagrams, drawings, lists, and boxed paragraphs supplement the text. Touches of color are added to most of the 7¾-by-10½-inch pages. The May issue publishes the annual index. A four-page brochure aids the teacher in using the monthly issues.

For students in grades six to eight, this monthly is likely to have particular value for its descriptions of numerous jobs and work clusters. Certainly the world of work should seem to offer many options to readers. For specific jobs, information and an overview are given about educational preparation, skills and requirements, tasks and responsibilities, and current opportunities in the labor market.   *Children's Magazine Guide*

Chickadee
Young Naturalist Foundation
Edit: 56 The Esplanade, Toronto, ON, M5E 1A7 Canada
Subs: P.O. Box 11314, Des Moines, IA 50340
Monthly; except July and August (10 issues)
$14.95; in Canada, $17

This highly pictorial, 32-page monthly aims to interest children up to the age of nine "in their environment and the world around them." Nature is the subject treated most frequently, although other sciences, in doses the young can handle, are not neglected. The unusually attractive illustrations—some color photographs are exceptional—are complemented by a particularly legible typeface. Issues customarily carry a fiction story to be read to the young child, but most pages present nonfiction and puzzles. The activities and games on the 8¼-by-10¾-inch pages include ones that subscribers are to fill in or mark up.

There is much to praise in this "Magazine for Young Children from OWL": the subject matter, the illustrations (and the variety of both) but most particularly the effect created by the frequent use of two-page spreads. Adjacent pages do not fight with each other for attention; readers can settle in on the opened pages, an element of design very appropriate for picture-book readers. Furthermore, the inclusion and placement of regular features and items introduce the young set to magazine conventions, especially the consistency of format.

Children can look for regular features. Inside the cover, a page-and-a-half color photograph launches each issue. An adventure tale related to the previous pages is told as a picture story; six fine watercolor paintings have under them sentences that some beginning readers could handle. The centerfold is always a pullout poster. Faithful subscribers should have an unrivaled collection of animals in close-up. In just three issues, the cover, initial feature, and centerfold offer an ocelot, a greatly magnified leap frog, a polar bear, the neck of a giraffe with three oxpeckers, arctic fox pups, and a hermit crab—all spectacular. Other pages bring colorful puzzles (color, match, find, identify, finish) especially suitable for the intended audience.

Four other features commonly appear. "Try this experiment with Dr. Zed" by its title invites the young one to participate in a simple science experiment with the jolly scientist of bow tie and sneakers and the child pictured in a close-up photograph. Instructions are clearly stated and easy to follow; materials are readily available. "What Happens?" in the experiment is explained in boxes on the pages. On four pages at the back of an issue are reproduced the artwork submissions from children, typically in response to a call for something specific (drawings of babies, of things that begin with the letter "j", and so on). The pages, all part of "Hoot," also carry photographs, letters, and brief stories from children. In one corner, a book is usually recommended. Another regular feature is the two-page cartoon "Daisy Dreamer," a freckle-faced girl with long plaits who happily engages in an exciting adventure in animal land before being awakened by Mom. The back cover shows six close-up photographs and asks "What is it?" In one issue, the viewer must decide which pet "owns" all of the items and in another must list the pairs (peanut butter and jelly, for example).

Among puzzles in three issues examined are those that require following lines or paths to get somewhere or make connections, matching items at the page's edge with the proper places in a picture, matching opposites, identifying like objects, unscrambling letters to form words, and eliminating objects that don't belong. The issues also bring a rebus letter puzzle and a beginning crossword puzzle. Instructions for crafts or activities include making a piñata and painting faces of jungle animals on hands. (Some children modeling the animals obviously relish letting the paint extend to the elbow to suggest the animal's body!)

Pictures are crucial in a work for young children, and this magazine succeeds admirably in exposing its subscribers to many types of illustration; and for each medium the publication offers superior if not striking work. The cover, when not carrying a photograph of a member of the animal kingdom, might host the winning illustration in the cover contest open to children age nine and under. The tone is set; the invitation is extended; the content does not disappoint. Any parent, grandparent, or teacher should be pleased for the opportunity to offer the adult guidance that will help the young "get the very most from their magazine."

Chickadee is available in a French-language version entitled *Coulicou* from Les Éditions Héritage Inc., 300 avenue Arran, Saint-Lambert, Quebec, J4K 1K5, Canada. The magazine is also published in Swedish, *Barnens*, and in Finnish, *Lasten Maailma.* *Children's Magazine Guide*

Child Life
Children's Better Health Institute
Edit: Benjamin Franklin Literary & Medical Society, Inc., 1100 Waterway Blvd., P.O. Box 567, Indianapolis, IN 46206
Subs: P.O. Box 7133, Red Oak, IA 51591
Monthly; except bimonthly January–August (8 issues)
$11.95

Following upon *Jack and Jill*, this magazine is now intended for ages 9 to 11 (formerly 7 to 9); however, it remains to be seen how the difficulty and interest levels of the contents are upgraded. Emphasis here, as in the other five magazines of the publisher, is on health with special attention to nutrition and safety. An expansion of scope in recent years has allowed inclusion of seasonal material, information about the animal kingdom, and special series such as the one about occupations. Interspersed among the fiction stories and nonfiction articles are the puzzles, games, and activities readers have come to expect of this colorful and amusing 6½-by-9⅛-inch magazine.

The matter between the covers is grouped on the contents page under "For Your Health," "Stories and Articles," and "Special Features." The first category lists two regular columns: "Ask Dr. Cory," prepared by Cory SerVaas, M.D., the publisher, and "Body News," a two-page report composed of short items about "the latest on keeping yourself healthy." A recipe is usually listed here (for example, Healthy Holiday Candy) with at least one educative piece ("More Valuable Than Diamonds" about your teeth, for instance). Under "Stories and Articles," fiction has a slight edge over nonfiction in the six or so items listed. An issue often carries a humorous story, a folklike tale, and a story with realistic characters and situations, sometimes adventurous. Nonfiction ranges widely and has covered mountain climbing in the Himalayas and extinct animals. The cover drawing of cartoon characters in a recent issue is picked up on at the centerfold and in a one-page report on the creation of the cartoons.

The one- and two-page pieces, so popular with subscribers, are listed under "Special Features." Often seasonal in content, the word puzzles, hidden pictures, dot-to-dot revelations, mazes, and pages on which to draw or color are certain to amuse. Each issue usually describes something to make—a bird feeder or a kaleidoscope, for example. A humorous verse is generally allotted a page, and the continuing cartoon "Diane's Dinosaur" runs to two pages. Readers contribute to "Jokes and Riddles" and "Poet's Page."

The very nature of the content suggests that this 48-page magazine should project in its illustrations an image of variety and busyness. A few drawings accompanying the longer pieces are the work of perceptive illustrators, while other representations merely decorate the pages. Full color is used on two-thirds of the pages. Drawings and sketches make up most of the pictorial work; photographs are used only occasionally.

Children's Magazine Guide

Children's Album
    EGW Publishing Co.
    Edit: 1320 Galaxy Way, Concord, CA 94520
    Subs: P.O. Box 6086, Concord, CA 94524
    Bimonthly; $17.70

The cover reminds readers that this magazine carries "Children's Crafts and Creative Writings." (The bimonthly incorporated both *Butterflies*, verses by children, and *Children's Crafts*, projects prepared by adults for children.) In its 32 pages are published stories, poems, plays, book reviews, and artwork by children. Interspersed among the original submissions from children are craft projects, puzzles, and workbook pages. The editor indicates that in the near future "a workbook section will be emphasized." The 8⅛-by-10⅞-inch magazine is intended for ages 8 to 14.

The contents page under "Features" lists 15 or more items, all contributions from children. For each title, the child author is named. Not unexpectedly, there are more poems than stories. The latter seemingly never extend beyond two pages. Among the regular "Departments" are "CA Workbook" and "Write On!" which has offered suggestions about establishing scene, setting pace, and rewriting. "Pen Pals" records those readers seeking a connection. "Book Nook" carries the reviews. Among the projects of the "Crafts" section on the contents pages are ones describing flower arranging, woodworking, and stenciling. Two pages at the center are regularly captioned "Games & Puzzles," and here may be found crossword puzzles, anagrams, and other word games.

In addition to the artwork by children, drawings and decorations are added to some pages by staff artists and others. Apparently some of the four-color front covers are the work of free-lancers. The color drawings of the back covers are made by children. About a half dozen pages in every issue are in several colors or have a color background. Typically, the craft project is given prominence by color.

Children's Better Health Institute
Benjamin Franklin Literary & Medical Society, Inc.
> *Turtle Magazine for Preschool Kids*   ages 2–5
> *Humpty Dumpty's Magazine*   ages 4–6
> *Children's Playmate Magazine*   ages 6–8
> *Jack and Jill*   ages 7–10
> *Child Life*   ages 9–11
> *Children's Digest*   preteen

The goal of all of these magazines is "to provide children with good reading that not only entertains but also educates, primarily about good health." Attention is given to safety, exercise, and nutrition. Beyond health there are articles about science, particularly nature study; fiction stories, realistic or adventurous; and articles and stories about seasons and holidays.

Readily recognized as members of the same publishing family, each magazine is 6½ by 9⅛ inches in size and contains 48 pages. An issue carries articles, stories, poems, and miscellanea, the latter including puzzles, games, recipes, jokes, riddles, cartoons, things to do and make, and contributions from readers. The differences in publications are related to targeted audience. While distinctions are not readily apparent where age levels overlap, the magazines for the youngest have more illustration than text. A gradual increase in reading difficulty can be noted, as well as a broadening of interests as the intended age level increases. To further the publisher's intent to incorporate "humor and a light approach," child characters and dialog are frequently introduced. The light and lively touch also prevails in the illustrations. Color is generously used in all magazines.

Children's Digest is made available in braille by the Library of Congress. *Jack and Jill* is available in braille and on audio disc recording.

Children's Digest
Children's Better Health Institute
Edit: Benjamin Franklin Literary & Medical Society, Inc., 1100
  Waterway Blvd., P.O. Box 567, Indianapolis, IN 46206
Subs: P.O. Box 7133, Red Oak, IA 51591
Monthly; except bimonthly January–August (8 issues)
$11.95

The top of the line with regard to targeted audience, this magazine, as all the publisher's others, is health oriented. Safety, nutrition, and exercise are overriding concerns of the publisher; however, within the magazine's scope are nature, science, sports, history, and biography. Nonfiction, fiction, games, puzzles, activities—all have bearing on the well being of children. Fiction in several forms (realistic stories, adventure tales, mysteries, and science fiction) is accepted from free-lancers, who are urged to keep the writing light and humorous. The 48-page magazine is now advertised for the preteen, following upon *Child Life*, which is for ages 9 to 11. Any change in the character of the magazine (it previously was intended for ages 8 to 10) is not yet evident.

On the contents page, the items of an issue are grouped under three headings: "Health"; "Stories, Features, & Activities"; and "From Our Readers." Six or more titles are listed in an issue under "Health." In a recent issue examined, one such title is a five-page fiction story about overcoming a fear of skiing. Two nonfiction articles under "Health" discuss, with humor, hiccups and teeth. A third mentions foods eaten around the world in celebration of the new year. These articles run two to four pages in length. The advice regularly given to children from the physician (and publisher) is printed in "Ask Doctor Cory." Two other items that are usually listed in this section are a recipe and a word puzzle.

Two other fiction stories of the issue examined are entered under "Stories, Features, & Activities." Here also is to be found two regular cartoon strips: "Mirthworms," with the same nine characters who also appear in *Jack and Jill*, and "Tim Tyme," about a boy who zips on a "timeboard" (skateboard) to other eras. "Book Beat" provides one-column reviews. Although there seemingly are not as many puzzles in this magazine as in others by the publisher, a dot-to-dot picture (with numbers going beyond 100) seems to make a regular appearance, and most issues have word puzzles but only occasionally a hidden-picture puzzle. Among the contributions from subscribers listed under "From Our Readers" are the regular items "Page of Poetry," "Jokes and Riddles," and "What Do You Think?" The last is composed of readers' letters about family, pets, hobbies, books, and so forth.

The magazine caters to the pictorial and presents a number of very ordinary drawings and cartoon-like illustrations in its 6½-by-9⅛-inch pages. Many of the puzzles and other pieces are short, each often filling only a single page. The typeface selected is one that furthers legibility, so that even though an overall impression of activity and movement is suggested, when settling into reading a few of the stories, the illustrations do not overwhelm or pull the eye unnecessarily from the text. Color brightens about two-thirds of the pages of every issue; full color is used on the cover. Three pages of full-color photographs can usually be counted in an issue. An edition in braille is made available by the Library of Congress.

Children's Magazine Guide

Children's Playmate Magazine
Children's Better Health Institute
Edit: Benjamin Franklin Literary & Medical Society, Inc., 1100
  Waterway Blvd., P.O. Box 567, Indianapolis, IN 46206
Subs: P.O. Box 7133, Red Oak, IA 51591
Monthly; except bimonthly January–August (8 issues)
$11.95

For the child growing along with magazines of this publisher, *Playmate* follows upon *Humpty Dumpty* and is intended for children ages six to eight. As with the other five titles from the Institute, this one is health oriented, emphasizing sensible health practices, regular exercise, and proper nutrition. The 48 pages, a mixture of stories, puzzles, and pictorial matter, are sorted on the contents page into two categories: "Health" and "More Fun." Seasonal tales and activities find a place in and among the health features.

Known for the variety offered between the covers, each issue contains about five prose pieces, with fiction stories usually outweighing articles by four to one; two poems, one long, one short; several regular pages, including contributions from subscribers; and eight or so puzzles, games, and activities. The fiction stories, about five pages in length, are apparently written by free-lancers. The vocabulary is manageable, and with a little assistance over troublesome spots, most beginning readers should be able to handle the lightweight narratives. Recent nonfiction pieces have considered mistletoe and skunks. The poem of each issue that runs to several pages is frequently strained, the fault often being in the attempt to combine fact with fun, wherein cadence and rhyme falter.

Children have the opportunity to contribute to several parts of the magazine that appear regularly. Verses about "good health, exercise, foods that are good for you, or safety" may be submitted to "Lines that Rhyme." More leeway, for lack of strictures, is given to the subject matter of artwork accepted for "Pictures by Our Playmates." Children are acknowledged as contributors to the joke part of "Jokes and Riddles" and the question part of "Ask Dr. Cory." Another regular item, not contributed by children, is "Jet & Rocket: Space-age Pals," a two-page comic strip about the zippy outer space excursions of two anthropomorphic characters.

The puzzles, as well as the crafts and recipes, often have a seasonal theme. Words and numbers are put to use in matching exercises, dot-to-dot pictures, and simple crossword puzzles and other word games. Hidden pictures and mazes train the eye and mind. Suggestions about things to do and items to make (including recipes) are usually appropriate to the time of year. Instructions are simple but not vague and sometimes allow for creative variations. In one issue, on one page are suggested three games to play in the snow, and on the adjacent page, ideas are presented for making snow statues representing an Eskimo village (although the penguin would be out of place there).

In illustration too there is much variety within an issue with regard to both style and quality. Among the finest and yet most diverse works are the drawings composed of strong and simple lines that capture their subjects in a few strokes and the drawings composed of sensitive details that allow feelings and emotions to be conveyed. However, much lies between the two types of drawings; the cartoon-like drawings will have popular appeal. Illustrators are often credited with the work accompanying stories and verses. Even though the names are different, the artwork suggests that the artists either are from the same school or are fulfilling specifications. Full color is used on the cover and about half the pages within. About 20 of the 6½-by-9⅛-inch pages are without color.

Children's Magazine Guide

Children's Television Workshop

> *Sesame Street Magazine*   ages 2–6
> *Kid City*   ages 6–10
> *3-2-1 Contact*   ages 8–14

Prepared in conjunction with television programs for children, the magazine formats listed above reflect, as much as possible, the fast-paced screen. Emphasizing the visual and the animated, the lively, fully illustrated pages, all in bright color, present innumerable suggestions of ways children might, with pleasure, improve their reading, math, and thinking skills. One- and two-page pieces aim to involve the reader and often include instructions about cutting out, filling in, or coloring. The magazines are easily recognizable as kin, each about 8 by 11 inches, but *Kid City* is "for graduates of *Sesame Street*," and *3-2-1 Contact* specializes in science and technology. Intended for an older and broader age range than the other two magazines, *3-2-1 Contact* has lengthier textual material and makes more use of photographs.

Choices see *Scholastic Choices*

Chuckles

> **Troll Associates**
> 100 Corporate Dr., Mahwah, NJ 07430
> 8 issues a year
> $9.95

Launched in 1988, this brightly colored magazine announces under its nameplate that it is "A First Magazine for Kids." Meant to be entertaining and educational for ages four to seven, the content of the two dozen pages is created at the editorial offices. Characters in pictures and puzzles are more often than not anthropomorphic. Energetic animals in vividly colored drawings seemingly jump out of the pages to smile at readers. Sprinkles (a puppy) and Kitty appear on the cover and lead the subscribers through many hilarious activities. "Chuckles" might be an understatement.

Among regularly appearing features are a three- or four-page read-to-me story and a few pages of full-color photographs of members of the animal kingdom. Swans, penguins, chipmunks, raccoons, and beavers, as well as animals that hibernate, have been beautifully pictured. Seasonal and holiday items are often presented. Reading and reading-readiness games make use of the alphabet. Sometimes a rebus story is included. Number puzzles develop beginning math skills. Challenges relevant to colors and shapes train the reader's eye and mind. Quite a few activities require matching, but there are also dot-to-dot pictures, simple mazes, and hidden-picture pages. Easy crafts and projects are suggested; some pages are meant to be colored or cut out. Riddles and board games too would be found in a year's subscription.

Wraparounds of the 8⅜-by-10⅞-inch issues contain a one-page note to parents and teachers about using the contents. Two months are named with publication date on issues examined, suggesting that the title is bimonthly for at least half the year.

Citizen see *Scholastic News: Citizen*

Classical Calliope see *Calliope*

Clavier's Piano Explorer see *Piano Explorer*

Cobblestone
    Cobblestone Publishing, Inc.
    30 Grove St., Peterborough, NH 03458
    Monthly
    $22.95; $14 each for 5 or more subscriptions to same address
A theme centering on an event or a period, an individual or people, a place, or a selected topic is explored in each issue of "The History Magazine for Young People"; this allows the articles to focus on the subject from several angles. The writing is noteworthy for its forthright and engaging style; there is neither condescension nor straining to amuse. Photographs, paintings, and other illustrations, many from holdings of museums and historical societies, illuminate the engrossing articles. The contents page lists the two major divisions of the material: "Features," listing about 10, and "Departments," citing about a half dozen. Wrapped in the full-color reproduction of the cover, the 7-by-9-inch pages within are so carefully arranged and white space is used to such advantage that the lack of color is hardly noticeable. The intent of the founders, to make U.S. history enjoyable, is understood at first glance. Although the 48-page magazine is intended for ages 9 to 15, anyone with the slightest curiosity about the history of America will find the monthly absorbing.

A list of the themes of the twelve 1989 issues should confirm the editors' breadth of vision and their ability to choose shrewdly from the spectrum of the past: "Children Who Shaped History," "Frederick Douglass: Fighter for Freedom," "Important Supreme Court Cases," "Hispanic Americans," "Entrepreneurs of the Past," "People with Disabilities," "Diné: The People of the Navajo Nation," "Environmentalism," "Thomas Jefferson," "Tuning In to Television," "Pilgrims to a New World," and "Norman Rockwell." Although the theme is linked to a date in the month, the issues offer worthwhile reading at any time. Back issues (1980 and on) are still available ($3.95 each) and would be a good buy for most libraries and many homes. A cumulative index covering 1980 through 1989 may be purchased for $6.95.

While the choice of themes is praiseworthy and unique in the field of children's magazines, the periodical ranks exceptionally for the way these themes are carried out. Not a hodgepodge of contributions, the content of each issue is arranged rationally, enabling the reader to proceed logically in and around the subject. Oftentimes meshing the progression from major topic to subheadings with a chronological approach, and always subscribing to the premise that people "make" history, the editors have developed packages that contain enlightening articles complemented by biographical and fictional pieces. The reader is supplied with fitting digressions and changes of pace in the artwork and activities. Consulting editors, authorities on the subject, are appointed for each issue, undoubtedly valuable members of the publishing team. The articles, far from being bland retellings, are peppered with specifics and particulars; and in detail, as well as through overview, the effort to attain accuracy in explanations, data, and terminology is obvious.

A close look at the articles in one issue might demonstrate how a theme is treated and how variety in content and presentation is achieved. For January 1990, the subject of history itself was chosen as the theme, an inspired choice because the magazine was celebrating its 10th birthday. That history is a personal ("everyone has a history") as well as a universal subject is conveyed early on in the letters to the magazine from children about their 10th birthdays, answers to the call for contributions that was voiced six months earlier. The two-page introductory piece asks "What Is History?" and brings together the many facets and fascinations of the subject that will be touched upon in the issue. The initial article uses for its title the Lincoln quote "We Cannot Escape History" and begins with early art and writing and with definitions of the word *history* but quickly moves to the work of historians and their skills, tasks, and training. Other sections of the article deal with primary sources, history in fiction stories, and oral history. A two-page spread of famous historians, "Elsewhere," provides a brief paragraph for each of seven, from Herodotus to Barbara Tuchman. In "Tales Around the Campfire," the pace and format change to reveal how native Americans remember their past. The role of storytelling and the mixing of legend and lore with history are discussed. A striking portrait of Black Elk introduces the article. Within the piece are comments about how Indians were portrayed in writings that are in need of revision.

The next piece, "History for the Future," mentions time capsules briefly and then describes how children could prepare one. The National Archives and Library of Congress are featured in "Homes for Our Nation's History." From national to local, the next item is captioned "Community Quest" and offers ideas and procedures for investigating one's own town in "a historical scavenger hunt." In "Landmarks of History," the interest in the restoration of buildings across the country is noted. An 1855 photograph showing the untended Mount Vernon is contrasted with the view today. Mention is made of the interesting circumstances leading to restoration projects, including local efforts across the country to save homes and stores. "Living History" highlights museums in all parts of the United States, as well as the reconstructed villages and places where people can gain an understanding of the times. The last major article is an interview with the notable author of history books for children, Milton Meltzer. At the back of the issue are the results of a contest about favorite books, "The Best Reading in History"; the winning submissions really turn out to be reviews. The body of the issue ends with a two-page poem entitled "What If . . ." (what if all the folks who've changed the world had lived and died and never tried?).

Among the monthly regulars are the two characters who romp in the prefatory and end matter: the Colonel, a crow, and Ebenezer, an elderly character who wears buckle shoes. Ebenezer encourages children to send letters, drawings, poems, and items pertinent to upcoming themes to "Dear Ebenezer" located in the first part of the magazine. At the publication's back, the cartoon characters decorate "Digging Deeper," pages that suggest books, films, and places to visit, as well as articles in earlier issues of *Cobblestone* that are relevant to the theme at hand. "Cobblestone Corners" is a one-page cartoon strip in which both the Colonel and Ebenezer usually appear. Inside the back cover an "Event in History" is celebrated with an illustration and a paragraph or two.

Nearly half the magazine is pictorial. The subject matter includes individuals (portraits), places, and Americans at work and play. The media might be oil paintings, watercolors, lithographs, photographs, posters, and early advertisements. That the illustrations are always germane to the text is evidence that effort was expended in locating and selecting the reproductions. Drawings, diagrams, and maps supplement the text when needed. As mentioned earlier, the uncluttered layout suggests the work of a designer with a thorough understanding of how to use white space effectively, choose typeface, and place text and illustrations on a page.

If there are still abuses of history in schools, the kind that leave memories of dates and distaste, then *Cobblestone* should be given a chance. It is, indeed, a magazine that can be enjoyed by child and parents. Carolyn P. Yoder oversees a fine enterprise but needs the help of teachers and librarians to make the magazine known to children. (It is with regret that I hear of professionals dismissing *Cobblestone*—and all its fine qualities—for lack of color.) *Children's Magazine Guide*

Cobblestone Publishing, Inc.

> *Calliope*   ages 9–15
> *Cobblestone*   ages 9–15
> *Faces*   ages 9–15

The three unrivaled magazines of this publisher have much in common but differ primarily in chosen focus. *Calliope* explores world history;

Cobblestone, American history; and *Faces*, people of the world, cultures near and far. All are the same size, but more importantly, all are of the highest calibre. The writing is straightforward and engaging; the content is consistently authoritative. In each issue, a theme is developed with consummate skill by the editor and guest editors, and even the subscriber becomes involved in creating the mosaic of the issue, and its idea, through activities and reading. An emphasis on people is not limited to *Faces*; it is shown in the other two magazines that people make history and that the studying of people and their circumstances makes history fascinating.

In addition to the nonfiction articles that make up most of these magazines' content, issues bring fiction and an assortment of games, puzzles, and even recipes. By planning ahead in the editorial office, reader contributions are in keeping with an issue's theme. At the back of issues are recommendations about books, audiovisual materials, and places to visit. The illustrations show great variety. Photographs are used when appropriate. Reproductions of paintings, sculpture, and other forms of art explain and extend the text. The inviting and topical covers are presented in full color. Within, black-and-white is used to advantage, sometimes making details clear and other times transporting readers to far-off times and places.

Cumulative indexes for *Cobblestone* and *Faces* provide access to the issues of the past decade.

Co-ed see *Scholastic Choices*

Creative Kids
 GCT Inc.
 Edit: P.O. Box 6448, Mobile, AL 36660
 Subs: P.O. Box 637, Holmes, PA 19043
 Monthly: October–May (8 issues)
 $24

Contributions by "*g*ifted, *c*reative, and *t*alented youngsters" (the first letters of which make up the publisher's name) fill the 32 pages of this magazine. Brief stories and poems are the mainstay of the monthly; however, many pages carry other submissions: artwork, including cartoons; photography; reviews of books, games, and computer programs; puzzles and activities; crafts; plays; and music. The publisher indicates that the age range of the readership is 8 through 14, although the contributors in issues examined range in age from 5 to 18. Their efforts are classified on the contents page; every item is listed with the author's name. Thus, over 70 titles are packed into the page's three columns. In issues seen, the back cover lists under "Write Away, Right Away!" some 60 names and addresses (with birthdates and interests) of children, mostly between ages 10 and 13, wanting pen pals.

The content suggests the various veins and different idioms in which children choose to express themselves. Short stories might be humorous or serious, factual or imaginative. The double-page spread of 15 poems in one issue confirms the intent to publish work that represents the "ideas, questions, fears, concerns and pleasures" of children. Among the words in the titles are *love, laughter, feelings, dream, spiders, velvet, athletes,* and *trench diggers.* One perceptive poem is titled "Lonely Cries of Children"; one title connotes a religious sentiment, "I Am Grateful." Only a few of the poems rhyme. Most are quite impressive and make appropriate use of fresh imagery. Poets on this two-page spread are almost all between ages 9 and 13; girls outnumber boys three to two.

Full color is used on two to three sheets (four pages to a sheet) of an issue. Other pages are highlighted or backed with a single color; several colors are used in an issue. The drawings and photographs are primarily those by children. Black-and-white photographs of authors occasionally accompany their work. Drawings from the publisher caption or decorate some features and announcements. The typeface is dark and clear. The layout of most pages is quite attractive. Although pages appear full, the contributions are set apart and not crowded.

The editors do not offer much guidance about what constitutes superior writing, as some other magazines that publish children's work do, but the guidelines indicate they are "looking for the very best material we can find." Each issue is a miscellany, offering much variety in content, form and format of expression, style of writing, and quality. The 8½-by-11-inch monthly adds its particular identity to the options available among magazines that publish solely children's work.

Cricket
Carus Corp.
Edit: P.O. Box 300, Peru, IL 61354
Subs: P.O. Box 52961, Boulder, CO 80322
Monthly; $29.97

Published since 1973 and never wavering from its intent to deliver the very finest magazine for children ages 6 to 12 who like to read, *Cricket* continues to reign supreme among general-interest periodicals and far outranks many of the magazines produced for the young. Although often pegged as a literary magazine because of the high calibre of its content, in truth, every issue carries many features besides the imaginative writing. Nonfiction articles, puzzles, games, activities, recipes, jokes and riddles, cartoons, book reviews, and such regulars as "The Letterbox," "Cricket League," and "Old Cricket Says" also make up an issue. Poetry, folktales, and biography are usually represented. The fiction stories might be fantasy, science fiction, historical fiction, or modern realistic fiction. The story might be mysterious, humorous, adventurous, suspenseful, or tender. Each 80-page issue offers reprints from highly regarded books, as well as original submissions, or perhaps commissions, of the most respected writers and illustrators of children's books here and abroad.

The excellence of literary content is complemented by the many illustrations, often by notable illustrators, which add much variety and liveliness to every issue of the magazine. The covers, when spread, reveal the superb full-color artwork of outstanding illustrators. Recognized and budding artists furnish the illuminating, informative, and sometimes decorative black-on-white illustrations. The styles of illustration are varied but compatible; the illustrators use tools that produce black print to advantage. The layout of the pages is obviously carefully conceived. The eye is drawn to a page and then readily explores it. White space is used effectively; no page ever appears cluttered or slapped together. Typeface is clear, legible, and of a fitting size. Touches of a single color are tastefully added to practically every page in an issue.

Monthly issues do not have specified themes, but frequently a number of the pieces can be linked by their common subjects. To understand both the way topics are related to one another and the variety in text and illustration, consider the content of a recent February issue. On the front cover is framed the portrait of an elegant black woman in African dress by Jerry Pinkney, illustrator of so many fine books for children. Surrounded gracefully by carefully drawn African animals, including a snake whose body undulates along the bottom edge of the back cover, the elegant storyteller in yellow flowing dress and red turban stretches a spider web among the fingers of both hands. The back cover pictures within the same decorative frame (but smaller in size) a colorful spider in its web. The frames of the front and back portraits are set against lush tropical vegetation. There are really three pictures here: one on the front cover, one on the back, and one in the opened and flattened covers. All are mesmerizing; the artist at once conveys delicacy and strength—in the woman stretching the rectangular web, the eyes and heads of the animals, the large spider on its thin web. The wordless invitation of the covers hints of the fascinating material within. The table of contents is set against a stylized design, a white pattern on an earth tone that could represent a web but at the very least suggests a textile from Africa. Titles and authors of stories, poems, and other features are duly noted. Cricket has leapt from his perch on the magazine's nameplate to the contents page and settles momentarily by Ladybug next to the title of their regular cartoon.

Following the letters to the editor, the first entry in the body of the issue is the full page given over to the charming poem by Langston Hughes with verses that begin "Just because I loves you." Leo and Diane Dillon interpret the wings of a butterfly and the fluttering leaves of an aspen. The page announces without fanfare that in this month designated for commemorating black history (and also Valentine's Day), the issue will honor contributions of black Americans to children's books and feature some of the African heritage.

The issue's first story is a retelling of a Bantu folktale about Chief Makanda Mahlanu, presently transformed into a five-headed snake, who seeks a wife. He chooses the kind and caring daughter of a poor man, not the arrogant sister. Zanyana's love breaks the spell, and the monster becomes a handsome young man. Sensitive sepia drawings of the Bantu girls and sketches of the huts and monster accompany the story. A page of jokes about snakes, changing the pace, precedes an informative three-page article about the growing of millet in central Africa and the preparation of the grain for consumption. Distinctive, bold woodcuts picture the processes. The regular crossword puzzle, Ugly Bird's, takes rivers of the world as its theme. A story titled "Wilbur's Hat" by well-known children's author Julia Cunningham tells about a snake that loses his precious black top hat to a crow, but a company of woodland animals contrives to get the stovepipe back by making the most of the crow's weakness for alluring items. "Snake Snacks" describes a recipe for a crispy tidbit in the shape of a stretched-out snake.

A boy from the realm of myth is protagonist in "The Tale of Melampus" in which the boy's kindness to two tiny orphaned snakes is returned with the ability to understand the language of all flying and crawling creatures. The retelling emphasizes that Melampus is never lonely because of his companionship with garden animals; not much is made of his becoming a great soothsayer. An article about the magical qualities of rainbows, as believed all over the world, begins with the association of rainbows and snakes, the rainbow-snake beliefs, of the Shoshoni Indians and the rainbow snake Kalseru worshipped by the Aborigines of Australia. The rainbow of tradition is followed by a science experiment in which the primary colors are combined to make white and by a discussion of the spectrum and reflected color, all adapted from a book prepared for the Smithsonian Institution. Next, young and old can experiment with sibilating as they hiss through a nonsense verse about six Sicilian snakes and six Serbian serpents.

In a fiction story, "Snake in the Night," a scary incident with a rattler turns out to be a joke on Dan's mother. In another fiction piece, "Tilly Reckons with a Snake," the put-upon younger sister of two teasing brothers bravely kills the snake that has been after the eggs in the henhouse. A rope-jumping rhyme from *Honey, I Love, and Other Love Poems* by Eloise Greenfield is balanced by an illustration of two black girls happily jumping. (Is the rope in that position a rainbow?) A setting in the past (it's 1851, you're in a mansion with a dark cellar) is given to a mystery, "A Day Full of Secrets," which is continued in the next month's issue. Margaret Walker's homage to her grandmothers, "Lineage," is from her book *For My People*. The story of a lion and squirrel, dubbed "a tale from Cameroon," is retold by a Maasi now living in Canada. A biographical piece about the author follows the story. "The Chief on the Mountain" is based on a true story from southern Africa. In 1824, Moshwayshway led his suffering people to become a strong and wealthy nation through peace, wisdom, and kindness. Caroline Feller Bauer recommends books about Africa, and her selections are among the very best. The next to last story in the issue is about a family from Virginia that is living someplace in Africa for the year. The daughters yearn for a pet, so their father brings home a hedgehog. The question then is "What Do You Feed a Pine Cone?" An issue of stories and tales from Africa would be incomplete without one about that Peripatetic trickster Anansi the spider. The greedy one gets his due from Turtle.

Cricket and an assortment of little critters roam the margins of the 7-by-9-inch pages, adding humor, giving background information and helpful commentary, or asking questions about the articles and stories. The gang parades across the bottom of the letters-to-the-editor page, and their adventures or problems are often continued at the bottom of other pages. Each little bug has its own identity. Sluggo the snail is steady, sure, and reliable with a heart as big as all outdoors. Among the other silhouettes are Charlie and Crystal, Cricket's cousins; the ant aunts, Marianne and Anna; Mimi the spider, secretary, and librarian; and the English Muffin, a British beetle.

Among the regular features are the contributions by children. "The Letterbox" publishes letters to "Dear Everybuggy," Cricket, Zoot, or anyone else. The subscribers themselves are an interesting and creative lot to judge by their letters. As in adult magazines, these pages provide entertaining reading. "Cricket League" reproduces the winning entries of poetry, story, and drawing contests, the subject of each suggested by the contents of previous issues. Instructions for the contests coming out of the current issue are outlined.

Marianne Carus has edited *Cricket* since its inception, and undoubtedly her high standards and persuasive influence have given direction to the magazine, a guidance that has kept the monthly a first-class publication. In addition to developing a taste in the young for quality literature and art, the intent is to present content in a lively, entertaining, and cheerful manner. Members of the editorial board are well known for their contributions to the study and promotion of the best in children's literature: Lloyd Alexander, Eleanor Cameron, Virginia Hamilton, Isaac Bashevis Singer, Ann Thwaite, and Jim Trelease, to name half the board.

An index is available covering the first 15 volumes (1973–1988).

Children's Magazine Guide

Current Consumer & Lifestudies
Field Publications
Edit: Curriculum Innovations Group, 60 Revere Dr., Northbrook, IL 60062
Subs: 4343 Equity Dr., Columbus, OH 43228
Monthly during school year: September–May (9 issues)
$15.95; $6.25 each for 15 or more subscriptions to same address

The publisher intends this classroom periodical for grades 7 to 12, a range that covers a great change in interests. By and large, this monthly is likely to be of greater value to those beyond grades 7 and 8. While some magazines for junior high are useful in upper elementary grades, this one carries quite a few articles that will have little attraction for children—choosing a college, insurance needs, and parenting, for example. Parts of the magazine might be useful to some junior high students. The articles that call upon the readers to weigh certain matters might well be considered by students below grade 9. Personal interests and needs, as well as institutional needs, will have to be assessed in light of this periodical's scope.

The publisher outlines in a grid the subjects and specific topics covered in a year's issues. The broad subject headings include "Family Matters," about being a member of a family; "Spotlight on You," a close look at oneself and relationships with others; and "Insight," survival skills and real-life issues. Three other headings are "Food Thoughts," guides to eating and cooking; "Clothes Closet," about buying, wearing, and caring for apparel; and "Dollars & Sense," about handling money and buying goods and services. The lengthy focus articles, introduced on the cover, take an in-depth look at topics of concern and have discussed the global environment, creative computing, dating decisions, and setting personal and financial goals. The articles of other categories are usually three pages in length. Among the regular columns are "Answering Service," a one-paragraph problem followed by a solution, and "Fun & Games," puzzles with answers on the contents page.

The writing is clear and straightforward in "The Practical Guide to Real Life Issues," the magazine's subtitle. Paragraphs are kept short. The subject matter is handled competently. The format of the 32-page, 7¾-by-10½-inch magazine is attractive; pages are not cluttered. Black-and-white photographs, drawings, and charts accompany articles. A brochure, "Teacher's Edition," is made available with group subscriptions. The May issue indexes the year's articles. The magazine succeeds well in fulfilling its intent. Children ready to move on from *Penny Power* (titled *Zillions* after August 1990) will find in this monthly much to consider about life and consumption.

Current Events
Field Publications
Edit: 245 Long Hill Rd., Middletown, CT 06457
Subs: 4343 Equity Dr., Columbus, OH 43228
Weekly during school year (26 issues)
$11.98; $5.99 each for 10 or more subscriptions to same address

For nearly 90 years, this newspaper has brought current events to the classrooms of America. Intended for grades 6 through 10, the newsprint four-page weekly presents coverage of world and national events and the people making these events in a vocabulary and style tailored to the reading abilities of grades 5 through 7. News reports and special features are designed to help social studies teachers meet curriculum objectives while teaching students how to read in content areas that make up the social studies. The front-page stories report happenings still very much in the news of adult papers; the reports are concluded on the second page. The center pages typically carry "Focus on the News," "News Briefs," and the Garfield cartoon. The back page offers "News Skills" and "News Crosswords."

Special four-page reports are inserted periodically. One proposes ideas about the world of 2090; another discusses the status of world communism. Front-page headlines in recent issues announce "Dark Days for Dictators" and a report on high school Bible clubs. "Focus on the News," boxed in the lower left corner of page two, gives some historical background relevant to the front-page stories. "News Briefs" of page three in issues examined covers concisely a variety of topics: hypothermia along with preventive measures, deposing a head of state, controversies over bison herds in Yellowstone, and new discoveries about dinosaurs. Among the exercises printed regularly on the skills pages are those dealing with "Understanding the News" (comprehension) and "News Vocabulary." Other exercises sharpen the skills necessary to read maps, charts, and graphs.

The 8⅛-by-11⅜-inch weekly, billed as "America's First School Newspaper" (since 1902), divides most news pages into four columns, suggesting the format of adult dailies. The top half of the front page is usually pictorial, making use of one or two photographs. Black-and-white photographs are the prime form of illustration; drawings brighten a few articles. A single touch of color is added to each issue, usually to highlight captions.

A guide for teachers suggests ways to use the newspaper and includes pages that can be reproduced for distribution to classes. The newspaper enables teachers to apply concepts of the social studies curriculum to events and people in the news. If not ordered in the classroom, *Current Events* might well be purchased in the home where help is needed in developing a child's skills and habit of daily newspaper reading.

Children's Magazine Guide

Current Health 1
Field Publications
Edit: Curriculum Innovations Group, 60 Revere Dr., Northbrook, IL 60062

Subs: 4343 Equity Dr., Columbus, OH 43228

Monthly during school year: September–May (9 issues)

$15.95; $6.25 each for 15 or more subscriptions to same address

A health magazine intended for students in grades four to seven, this classroom monthly is well worth home and library subscriptions, especially for children who might not be introduced to this fine magazine in their classrooms. "The Beginning Guide to Health Education" (its subtitle) regularly presents articles under certain broad headings. The major areas addressed in each issue are: "Nutrition," "Drugs," "First Aid and Safety," "Psychology," "Disease," "Fitness and Exercise," and "Personal Health." "Your Healthy Environment" is included in most but not all monthly issues. The first article in each issue is a feature that is introduced on the full-color cover. "Stethoscope" reports recent health news. "Funny Bone" and "The Sunny Side" provide riddles, word games, and other amusements. Subscribers will find the answers to their questions about health matters in "Just Ask Us."

The editors seemingly encourage children to take health seriously, yet the magazine does not succumb to being sober or fear inducing. The writing is forthright and a fitting contrast to health magazines that make the subject all too jolly. The articles are informative, giving facts and exploring possibilities. The authors take into account that their subjects might be relatively new to the young, but in early paragraphs, they relate the topics to the child's world and then quickly begin using the correct terminology. Definitions and pronunciations help the reader tackle words that won't be found on an easy-vocabulary list, for example, anorexia nervosa. Charts and diagrams help explain the text. Black-and-white photographs accompany many articles. Touches of a color are added to most pages.

Among the cover-page features in one year are articles about nutrition goals for the year 2000 and technology and research of the future, as well as articles about wellness, self-esteem, the brain, skin, the endocrine system, and sports medicine. These feature articles often run to eight pages and provide fine coverage of the subject. The other articles in an issue are two to three pages in length. Each falls under one of the major areas of the topic outline, a grid the magazine has used for several years.

Under the category of psychology in one year there are articles about dysfunctional families, shyness, rejection, hypochondria, suicide, and fears and phobias. Both abuse and drug use are discussed in the course of a year in articles about refusal skills, hallucinogens, food and drug interactions, allergy medications, and prescription know-how. Articles about diseases treat the afflictions' symptoms, manifestations, and treatments in an objective but understanding tone. Among the first aid and safety articles, in addition to those about athletic injuries and scratches, itches, and burns, have been a guide for babysitting and information on a Red Cross program for children. Exercises and sports, especially those that meet objectives of fitness rather than competition, are described regularly.

A recent February issue quite appropriately features a large, red appleheart on the cover with the lead story titled, "Do Your Heart Good." Within seven pages, information about the circulatory system, heart diseases, and cholesterol is presented, always in a manner that children can grasp and relate to their own heart and body. The vocabulary building alone is impressive: polyunsaturated, septum, and mitral, to name some of the words explained and for which pronunciations are given. Other articles in this same issue consider gateway drugs (alcohol and tobacco), diabetes, making friends, and how four recent presidents have handled illness and health. The four-page nutrition article stars the potato—its history, nutrients, and three recipes. In "Just Ask Us," five letters from subscribers are answered, including questions about acrophobia and diverticulitis. A crossword puzzle features words with a heart connection.

The 32-page monthly, printed on semiglossy paper, is attractive and inviting in layout. Pages are arranged in various patterns. Text is placed in three columns on the 7¾-by-10½-inch pages. On the contents page, the topic area is printed in boldface; under it, the title of the article is given. Authors are not identified on the contents page or at the articles; presumably staff editors, writers, and consultants are responsible for copy. An index appears in the May issue. A four-page brochure for teachers offers ideas for extending the content of an issue, suggesting questions to raise and activities to try.

Many children have a natural curiosity about matters of health. No other magazine for children in upper elementary grades treats the subject so thoroughly and honestly. The broad coverage of topics and the articles of the monthly issues should satisfy the inquisitiveness of the young. Subjects that some magazines shy away from or sugar-coat are featured with respect and integrity here. This writer has no difficulty prescribing a subscription.   *Children's Magazine Guide*

Current Health 2
Field Publications
Edit: Curriculum Innovations Group, 60 Revere Dr., Northbrook, IL 60062

Subs: 4343 Equity Dr., Columbus, OH 43228

Monthly during school year: September–May (9 issues)

$15.95; $6.25 each for 15 or more subscriptions to same address

"The Continuing Guide to Health Education" (the magazine's subtitle) is the older sibling of *Current Health 1*. Intended for grades 7 to 12, the monthly covers the same broad subject areas as the magazine for younger children, but the discussions here are in keeping with the abilities and interests of adolescents. The lengthy lead article is always introduced on the full-color cover. The rest of the topics are suitably treated in two- and three-page articles. Regular columns that carry the same captions as those in the magazine for elementary grades are "Stethoscope" and "Just Ask Us." "The Sunny Side" on the back cover uses a crossword puzzle or another word game to quiz readers on the content. The 32-page monthly is suitably illustrated with black-and-white photographs and drawings. Touches of color are added to many pages.

Some of the topics discussed in the feature articles of one year are alcohol, self-esteem, healthy eating, pain, and sleep. Among the wide variety of articles under the eight subject areas of the magazine's annual grid of coverage are those about rheumatic fever, lupus, cocaine, everyday addictions, salt and fat, contact lenses, hearing, choking, muscle cramps, recreational sports, schizophrenia, and preparing for exams. Not meant to frighten, the articles outline facts and situations with an almost clinical objectivity but often end with urging students to choose (when a choice is available) in favor of good health and safety habits. Some of the articles carry the same basic content as those in *Current Health 1,* but interest and reading levels are upgraded for the older targeted audience.

The monthly is published for children in two of the grade levels within this book's scope (seven and eight) but also serves students through senior high. Individual subscribers have the option of choosing either *Current Health 1* or *2* according to their particular needs. No mention of grade levels is made within the issues themselves. A four-page leaflet for teachers provides questions, activities, and answers to puzzles. An optional supplement on human sexuality is available with a subscription to *Current Health 2* for an additional payment. Sex education topics are discussed in the four-page supplement in an open and forthright manner.

Current Science
Field Publications
Edit: 245 Long Hill Rd., Middletown, CT 06457

Subs: 4343 Equity Dr., Columbus, OH 43228

Biweekly during school year (18 issues)

$11.98; $5.99 each for 10 or more subscriptions to same address

A biweekly that alerts students in grades 6 to 10 (reading levels five through seven) to news in the sciences, this 16-page classroom periodical reports recent developments in earth, physical, and life sciences. A special point is made of covering health; news that doesn't fit neatly elsewhere is captioned "General Science." With about half the space of each issue given over to illustrations, the magazine has browsing appeal. Even so, young people's interest in science should draw many to the publication. The full-color full-page cover photograph beckons readers, in part by the quality of its reproduction but also for its subject and composition. The writing within is clear and solid.

The initial one-page story to the right of the contents page in the three consecutive issues examined is undoubtedly meant to be an attention grabber. Among the startling titles are "Snake Cleans Owl's Home" and "Error Found in New Dinosaur Stamp." Other articles are slotted in the contents page under the appropriate science; each category is represented in an issue. "Earth Science News" in various issues has carried articles on earthquakes, beach erosion, and the ice age. Physical science has covered the uses of solar power, an encyclopedia on compact disc, and new devices for tracking stolen cars. Among the news items in the life sciences are those about endangered species, behavior of pets, and the findings of a study of a beaver colony. Health news reports recent studies about diseases and afflictions, including emotional ones, and makes known that "New Defenses Against Common Cold Found." Usually two of an issue's science reports are reported on a two-page spread; the rest are one page in length. Beyond these reports, a controversial topic is sometimes introduced along with various points of view.

The back cover of each issue shows full-color "Mystery Photos," often enlargements to be identified. (Answers are provided only in the teacher's guide.) The last four pages of every issue carry the "Science News Briefs" in a four-column layout with accompanying illustrations. The subjects range widely but certainly are of contemporary interest; some are downright intriguing. Some issues bring an "Activity" page, which is usually a quiz that might require recall or thinking.

The magazine uses full color on about half its pages and a single color for highlighting the rest. The variety of illustrations is an important facet of this biweekly. In addition to the many photographs (black and white and color), there are drawings, diagrams, maps, charts, graphs, cartoons, and cross-sectional views. The choices suitably fit the purposes. Illustrative matter extends the text.

A four-page guide for teachers supplies a summary of each article's content and questions for discussion. Pages that can be reproduced for classroom distribution have exercises for developing skills, particularly in vocabulary and critical reading of science materials. This guide has an annual index in the last issue of the school year.

Much of the copy presented in the biweekly is too recent to be in textbooks, and it is this informative and interesting matter that makes science so fascinating. Although this magazine, now in its sixth decade of continuous publication, is intended for teacher-directed use in junior high classrooms, the best parts of issues will need no introduction, not even to younger students.   *Children's Magazine Guide*

Curriculum Innovations Group
> *Current Health 1*   grades 4–7
> *Current Health 2*   grades 7–12
> *Career World*   grades 6–12
> *Current Consumer & Lifestudies*   grades 7–12
> *Writing!*   grades 7–12

Curriculum Innovations Group is now a component of Field Publications. With the exception of *Current Health 1,* these magazines are primarily intended for secondary school classrooms. *Writing!* might well be considered for libraries serving children in upper elementary grades, and some children in these grades might want personal, or home, subscriptions. The other three magazines, leaning toward adolescent and even adult interests, would be of less usefulness in elementary schools (not an intent of the publisher anyhow) but should be considered by libraries serving junior high students and by parents and teachers who want to make subscriptions available to youngsters.

These five classroom periodicals, although different in content, have a number of similarities. Each is a 32-page monthly (during the school year) with a full-color cover and is printed on semiglossy 7¾-by-10½-inch pages. Major areas of emphasis are identified for the school year for each magazine, and these are highlighted regularly on the contents page. The first article, and the longest, focuses on a special subject; the remaining articles, as many as eight, address the subjects of emphasis outlined for the periodical. A few humorous and exercise activities are included in each issue. An index for the year is published in the May issue. The writing is usually straightforward and not at all condescending. The layout is attractive; photographs, drawings, and color complement the well-arranged text. Four-page teachers' editions are available.

Daybreak Star
> **United Indians of All Tribes**
> 1945 Yale Place East, Seattle, WA 98102
> Monthly during school year: October–May (8 issues)
> $16; $5.75 each for 5 or more subscriptions to same address; $24
>   for libraries

The monthly issues of this 24-page newsprint magazine are about Indians of the United States and Canada. Particular regions are featured in seven of the issues; the eighth and last issue of a school year is filled entirely with contributions from children. The subscription rates favor bulk orders, and the magazine is probably meant primarily for classrooms. Intended for grades three through seven, the tone of the publication is encapsulated in the phrase of the masthead, "the herb of understanding." The eight-pointed Daybreak Star, not necessarily herbaceous, comes from the Great Spirit and imparts understanding.

In specific articles and within the content as a whole, emphasis is placed upon "ancient days, modern ways." Among the areas focused upon recently, although other regions are treated in turn, are the Far North, Eastern Woodlands, Great Plains, and Southeast. Each issue brings both an informative article about the culture (the life and customs) of the Indians of the featured region and a legend. Other articles deal with natural history and sometimes nature study specifically.

Crafts and activities provide suggestions of things children might do. The back page offers review questions. A variety of puzzles lightens the pages. A crossword puzzle and a Seek & Find (hidden words in a square of many letters) seem certain to appear. The cover drawings are particularly captivating. Illustrations, both decorative and explanatory, consist primarily of drawings, sometimes of symbols. A single touch of color is added to the 8¼-by-10¾-inch pages of each issue.

The issue composed of contributions from children showcases artwork, verses, puzzles, informative pieces, the retelling of legends, and brief stories, sometimes about personal experiences. This is a particularly engaging issue, as is the work of Indian children in other issues. In the first seven issues, students of a particular school sometimes provide copy for several pages.

Although an intent of this magazine (which can be considered a little press publication) is probably to allow Indians to share experiences, there is much that others might learn from the pages. Certainly the expressions of today's children in artwork and writing are compelling, whether the leanings are toward honesty or humor.

Disney's DuckTales Magazine
Welsh Publishing Group, Inc.
Edit: 300 Madison Ave., New York, NY 10017
Subs: P.O. Box 11266, Des Moines, IA 50340
Quarterly; $7.80

This full-color magazine features the characters of the *DuckTales* television show, and its cover as well as its centerfold poster usually show Uncle Scrooge and Louie, Huey, and Dewey in some sort of odd predicament. Webby, the young female, sometimes joins them. On the contents page, about five titles are listed under "Features." Six to eight entries are named under "Departments." The quarterly, first published in 1988, is highly pictorial and intended for children ages 8 to 12. The lively antics of the major characters are sketched on most of the 32 pages, the exceptions being those pages carrying ads for Disney movies and products, and cereals, which often use strip cartoons. Hilarious fun, consternation, and excitement prevail.

Among the regular columns, the world's richest duck introduces the issue in "Uncle Scrooge's News," and letters and other reader contributions are printed in "Deliveries to Duckburg." "What's Quackin'" alerts readers to the latest videos, movies, television shows, and books, as well as to new attractions at theme parks. "Really Weird Inventions from Gyro's Brainstorming Barn" introduces the young to contraptions à la Rube Goldberg for such tasks as making sandwiches, taking care of a dog, and shoveling snow. "Draw a Duck" shows on a grid the sequential steps in drawing one of the cartoon characters, not always a duck. At the back of an issue, a collection of jokes from the fellows with "lots of time to kill in prison" is captioned "Beagle Boys Belly Laughs."

Each issue runs two "original DuckTales stories." One is a four-page cartoon strip; the other is a three-page adventure told in words and paragraphs. In issues examined, the continuing feature "Round the World with the Junior Woodchucks" took readers on trips to see African animals, spring training in Florida, and Alaska. Full-color photographs show the geographic locations; the cartoon characters are superimposed on the pictures. Some nonfiction articles have featured the U.S. Mint and the little-known inventors of commonly used items. Issues are rounded out with puzzles (word and number) and simple board games. With the exceptions already noted, most pieces are a page or two in length.

Disney's Mickey Mouse see *Mickey Mouse Magazine*

Dolphin Log
The Cousteau Society, Inc.
Edit: 8440 Santa Monica Blvd., Los Angeles, CA 90069
Subs: 930 W. 21st St., Norfolk, VA 23517
Bimonthly; $10

The global water system provides the connections for the articles about all forms of water life and the reports of people who have studied and explored that domain. The full-color bimonthly, intended for ages 7 to 15, probes areas of science, history, and even the arts, as they relate to the water system. Emphasis is, however, on marine biology, ecology, natural history, and the environment. Full-color photographs are found throughout the 16 pages of an issue, including the covers. Some photographs are particularly striking and would intrigue viewers of any age.

About five two-page articles appear in an issue, more than half the space allotted to pictorial matter. Although the text is undoubtedly edited with the young reader in mind, precise terms are not compromised. For this, the editors deserve praise. The text reads quite easily, and save for the very youngest in the targeted audience, children will be able to handle it on their own. The articles in one issue feature the returning of captured fish and animals to the ocean, puffers, a visit to an underwater cave of an island off Borneo, and seven of the world's best "inventions" that existed in nature long before used by people (jet propulsion, for example).

A maze follows the article about the dark underwater cave. The crew of the Calypso rescued some trapped sea turtles; in the maze, not only the route to the turtle must be found, but the number of minutes on various paths must be added up. The articles, quizzes, and puzzles of another issue treat icebergs, the blue whale, and storms originating at sea. On one page, superlatives are presented (largest island, and so on) and on another, special characteristics of specific members of the animal kingdom (the albatross has the longest wing span, for example).

A regular column at the front of an issue is "News from . . ."—an expedition, Calypso, Paris, and so forth. In the back, "Nature News" reports brief items within the magazine's scope. Inside the back cover, "You and Yours" is a page of miscellaneous items, including letters from subscribers, activities to participate in or try, and curious phenomena under "Did You Know?" Front and back covers usually carry splendid full-color photographs, occasionally a drawing, mostly of inhabitants of the water.

An intent of the magazine is to help children understand the interconnectedness of living organisms (including people); suggesting the links allows for a variety of topics. Understanding is meant to pave the way for an appreciation of the environment. The 8-by-10-inch bimonthly with its fascinating accounts of life in and around the sea provides a vehicle to "delight, instruct and instill" in these matters.

The magazine is one of the few of exceptional quality that parents too can fully enjoy when sharing its content with children. An individual subscription costs $10, which serves as an annual contribution to the Cousteau Society. A family membership, which includes *Calypso Log* (for adults) and *Dolphin Log*, is $28.

Plans call for increasing the number of pages to 20 and adding a cartoon adventure series. *Le Dauphin* is a 24-page edition published quarterly in France. *Children's Magazine Guide*

DuckTales see *Disney's DuckTales Magazine*

DynaMath see *Scholastic DynaMath*

Electric Company Magazine see *Kid City*

Explorer see *Scholastic News: Explorer*

Faces
> **Cobblestone Publishing, Inc.**
> 30 Grove St., Peterborough, NH 03458
> Monthly; except July and August
> $21.95; $12.95 each for 5 or more subscriptions to same address

The subtitle, "The Magazine about People," hints of the content of this anthropology and natural history magazine, published in cooperation with the American Museum of Natural History (New York) for children ages 9 to 15. Each issue centers on a many-faceted topic of import to human societies—past and present, here and anywhere. A half dozen informative and well-written articles develop the theme from a variety of perspectives. Black-and-white photographs and drawings help explain the narrative. The articles are written primarily by experts (to judge by the credentials given)—experts who know how to write for an intelligent child audience. Interspersed among the articles of an issue are usually three activities, things for children to do or make, one of which is a recipe. The magazine promises to take "young readers to far-off lands to experience the lives and cultures of people," and it does that exceedingly well.

The themes of a recent year attest to the magazine's breadth of scope as well as to the acumen of the editor in identifying topics with intriguing possibilities, topics that nevertheless can be comprehended by children.

Faraway places of theme trips include Brazil, Madagascar, and the Arctic. In one issue, farm children of four diverse cultures, as well as migrant workers, are featured and in another, puppets of North America, Europe, and Asia. "Rain: Key to Survival" is followed by "Importance of Iron." "People of the Forest" ventures to environments in Africa and South America, among other locations, where the forest is home and dictates livelihood and way of life. The October issue highlights "Witches and Wizards" of all times and all places in articles explaining people's beliefs about the supernatural.

In the same year noted above, the December issue highlights "The Glory of Gold." On the front cover is the striking and ever-enticing funeral mask of King Tut, full forward and vibrant in blue and gold. The contents page lists six articles (regularly captioned "Features"), three activities, and a half dozen departments, several of which appear monthly. In a two-page introduction, the editor prepares the reader for the content; featured places are marked on a world map. The opening sentence affirms the role of anthropology: "The brilliance and color of gold have long had a unique appeal to people everywhere." To begin by discussing here the six features, one of which is a folktale, would not convey the pacing of the issue. The activities, for example, are tucked among the articles, often appropriately coming out of a related topic. Therefore, it seems fitting to explore gold page by page.

The lead story discusses gold as a remarkable metal, "the supermetal," detailing its qualities from ore to gold leaf and the processes that lie between. A folktale from India about the golden stag teaches the way to wisdom. "The Gold of the Pharaohs" tells of the mines and goldsmiths of ancient Egypt and of magnificent jewelry and items of ritual, as well as the precious metal's magical properties that associate gold with gods. It is then time for a break to head to the kitchen with full instructions for baking from scratch a gold cake (lemon and egg yolks) topped with gold-dust icing. In a seven-page picture essay about the elegance of gold, children's author Robert D. San Souci provides the descriptions of the photographs. Within the mélange are spotlighted American coins, a Florentine cup, a Persian illuminated manuscript, the golden calf, a gilded dome, the jewelry of an Asante chief, a dragon robe from Tibet, and Bette Davis as Elizabeth I! Following this visual presentation are instructions for making a modern-day illuminated manuscript with felt-tip pens or crayons. The next two pieces take the reader to Peru. The first reports the incredible findings in the excavating of the Sipan tomb; the second shows how to make replicas of facial ornaments of ancient Peru from gold wrapping paper. The final feature explores alchemy, a discussion that is not limited to the Middle Ages.

The sentence on the back cover aptly sums up the gold issue: "Because of its beauty and scarcity, because it does not lose its luster, and because it can be easily fashioned into so many forms, gold has been specially valued since ancient times." Thus, the issue does have a strong underlying theme; the articles take readers to faraway times and places, and with reason.

Certainly the role of the editor is prime, and evident here. Diverse topics in an issue form a unit, not just a series of articles.

The activities in any issue are suitably demanding and stimulating for readers, and the instructions—pictorial and verbal—are sufficiently detailed. Games, recipes, and crafts are the typical fare. Among the games are those played in foreign countries, mazes and picture puzzles, and word puzzles that put to use the vocabulary of the issue. Recipes might be for baking or cooking, snacks or beverages. Crafts have required, among other materials, clay, paper, and wire.

Among the departments listed fairly regularly on the contents pages are those placed at the back of issues. "Further Exploring" recommends books and audiovisual materials. "*Faces* from the Past" notes earlier issues of the magazine that carry articles relevant to the theme at hand. "The Next *Faces*" announces the upcoming issue. "Letters and Drawings" publishes the submissions of children, including their poems.

Many of the articles' authors hold positions at museums and academic institutions. Free-lancers are advised that all work is commissioned on a by-assignment basis, although outlines for consideration are welcome. All manuscripts are reviewed by the American Museum of Natural History. The editorial process helps explain the authoritativeness of the articles. Further, writers are encouraged not to overlook the obvious yet to include little-known information.

Text and illustration, overall, are about equally proportioned in the 40 pages of an issue. The clear black-and-white illustrations fittingly complement the text, at once confirming and extending the narrative. The interplay of text and illustration is particularly noteworthy where details are to be observed. This magazine has a special responsibility to picture faithfully the unusual, the unfamiliar, and the ancient, which it fulfills quite laudably. A few original photographs are presented, but many of the illustrations are reproductions of works held by the natural history museums (and their libraries) of research and academic institutions. Some pictorial items are illustrations from books. Line drawings accompany some articles and most fiction pieces.

The full-color front covers of this 7-by-9-inch monthly are striking; sometimes the pictorial matter extends to the back covers. Most often color photographs of children from various parts of the world invite inspection of the issues. Nevertheless, within one year, cover status was also given to a Japanese woodblock print, a detail of a famous Spanish painting, and a Disney cartoon character.

Back issues of this magazine produced since 1984 (about 50 now) are presently available for $3.95 each. Because the material does not become easily dated, the back issues are certainly worth purchasing. The publisher will provide a list. These issues, like the current ones, should be respected as magazines (not books) and promoted for the special qualities of magazines that allow for variety in the content and its arrangement. An index covering October 1984 through June 1990 is available for $6.95.

Carolyn P. Yoder has been editor-in-chief from the outset and certainly deserves laurels for her dedication and persistence in wanting to introduce children to substantial topics through writing and illustration of the highest calibre at a time when the ephemeral brings the big bucks. In homes, libraries, and classrooms where adults want to expand the knowledge and vision of the young, *Faces* should find a welcome place. And there is more than enough for adults to learn from the magazine!

Children's Magazine Guide

Field Publications

Weekly Reader Pre-K Edition   prekindergarten
Weekly Reader Edition K   kindergarten
Weekly Reader Edition 1   grade 1
Weekly Reader Edition 2   grade 2
Weekly Reader Edition 3   grade 3
Weekly Reader Edition 4   grade 4
Weekly Reader Edition 5   grade 5
Weekly Reader Senior Edition   grade 6
Weekly Reader Summer Edition   grades K–5
U*S*Kids   ages 5–10
Know Your World Extra   grades 6–12; reading level grades 2–3
Current Events   grades 6–10; reading level grades 5–7
Current Science   grades 6–10; reading level grades 5–7
Read   grades 6–10; reading level grades 5.5–7

A line of classroom periodicals (except for *U*S*Kids*), this series does not extend as fully into senior high as does the Scholastic set. All the magazines are listed above. The ones for junior high are especially geared to students having difficulty with curricular subjects. The emphasis is on current events, aside from *U*S*Kids*, *Read* (language arts), and *Current Science*. News stories, articles, and photographs of people and happenings are meant to inform and develop newspaper habits and skills. From the few sentences describing a topic in the editions for lower grades to the lengthier explanations in the upper grade editions, the intent is to motivate children to read and develop various reading skills. All the magazines except *U*S*Kids* are published on newsprint and excluding the 32-page digest-sized *Read* are about 8 by 12 inches. *U*S*Kids*, printed on high-quality coated stock, uses full color throughout. Many pages in the other titles are presented in full color.

Weekly Reader Senior Edition is available in a large-print edition. *Weekly Reader* (Editions 2 through 5), *Current Events*, *Current Science*, and *Know Your World Extra* are available in braille and large-print editions. For current prices and availability, write American Printing House for the Blind, 1839 Frankfort Ave., Louisville, KY 40206.

Some titles are available in braille and large print. See Appendix B Editions for Visually Impaired.

Free Spirit
> **Free Spirit Publishing, Inc.**
> 123 N. Third St., Minneapolis, MN 55401
> Bimonthly during school year (5 issues)
> $10

Advice, information, and encouragement are offered children ages 10 to 14 about the problems and concerns of adolescence in this eight-page bimonthly of tabloid size. Emphasis is placed upon the social and emotional anxieties of growing up in today's world. Subtitled "News & Views on Growing Up" (the word *gifted* has been dropped), the magazine publishes only nonfiction. Authors, when not subscribers themselves, are educators, mental health professionals, and adolescent development experts. In the brief articles, questions are often posed, usually for self-analysis, or tips are enumerated. The prime audience is young people who are bright, talented, and creative. The intent is to provide help in managing stress and pressure, in getting along with family, friends, and teachers, and in handling high expectations.

Each issue centers on a theme. During one year the subjects were creativity, self-esteem, health, careers, and making a difference (ways for adolescents to make the world a better place). The issue about health embraces physical, social, and emotional well being. The front-page article by a clinical social worker titled "Sound Minds, Sound Bodies—Sounds Good!" packs in a great deal of information (and even some Latin). There is no condescension; actually, adolescents fare better than some adults in the commentary. The tone of the article is at once consoling, encouraging, and challenging. The article closes on the issue's last page with four tips for healthy living and two recommended books, one of which is reviewed on another page. The authors of a two-column article (from a book forthcoming from the magazine's publisher) advise keeping a daily happiness list of good feelings. Elsewhere in the issue are listed nearly 30 feel-good responses of subscribers to depression, frustration, or feeling blue. Four articles are by adolescents, the longest a first-person account of living with diabetes. Another 12-year-old writes briefly about the healthiest person she knows. Full-page coverage is given to resources (people and agencies) from which to seek factual information about drugs.

A survey of subscribers is initiated in the left column of the front page of each issue; findings are reported in subsequent issues where the topic is usually pertinent to the theme. Writing and cartoon contests of the magazine are announced, as well as a few contests and competitions for youths sponsored by other sources. The bottom half of the back page carries the cartoon-like characters of Douglas Jackson in "Severely, Profoundly and Inoperably Gifted!"

Few articles exceed a half page in length, which suggests that the newspaper format (although heavier paper stock is used) is compatible with the brevity of the content. Captions are printed in boldface of rather thick and rigid letters, and dark lines demarcate the four columns of a page. Drawings and a single color (different for various issues) lighten most sheets.

Subscribers are encouraged to submit nonfiction articles and interviews; however, their contributions appear more regularly in "Dear Judy," an advice column by editor-in-chief Judy Galbraith, and in "Letters to the Editors."

A supplement for teachers for the year's issues may be purchased through a separate subscription; free supplements are sent with classroom orders. The suggestions of a supplement examined filled both sides of a legal-sized sheet.

Games Junior

PSC Games Limited Partnership
Edit: 810 Seventh Ave., New York, NY 10019
Subs: P.O. Box 2082, Harlan, IA 51593
Bimonthly; $11.97

Junior is the offspring of a magazine meant to entertain readers while exercising their minds. From its first appearance in 1988, this bimonthly has offered in each issue plenty of puzzles to challenge children 6 to 12 years of age. While the magazine's primary intent is to be entertaining, the editors hope the games will, in addition, teach children to think in new and different ways.

The various and sundry amusements are grouped on the contents page into four categories: "Picture Puzzles," "Word Play," "Mystery, Logic, and Numbers," and "Games & Trivia." Consider the challenges of the first category in one particular issue: discovering objects in the ever-popular hidden-picture puzzle; coloring certain geometric shapes to reveal an animal or object; pinpointing mistakes in a zany full-page scene; figuring out literal drawings (bulldog); naming cartoon characters in tiny kaleidoscopic photographs; maneuvering from the top left of a double-page spread of 40 full-color beautiful stamps of birds, butterflies, and cats from many foreign countries to the bottom right; and a connect-the-dots page that upon completion makes a maze to negotiate.

The "Word Play" category too offers much variety and several levels of difficulty. Some puzzles give parts of words in need of letters, and in others, words are hidden among letters. Typical crossword puzzles are supplemented by word puzzles with clever twists, such as pictures for clues rather than words. The letters of one skillfully devised puzzle form a circle, with the clues of the outer edge suggesting words whose final letters begin the words related to the inner-circle clues.

Four items are listed under the "Mystery, Logic, and Numbers" heading. Among the regular entries is the two-page "Detective's Notebook" with its picture mystery (solve the crime by analyzing script and illustration), top secret (ideas for the would-be detective), and mystery riddle. Another regularly appearing item, for younger children, is "Out of Order," panels of a comic strip in need of unscrambling. If the logic problem can't be solved, the answer is at the back of the issue along with all the other answers. The last grouping, "Games & Trivia," includes reviews of new commercial games, especially board and card varieties. Multiple-choice quizzes test knowledge about early implements, inventors, and cats, to name some of the hardly trivial topics. Each issue provides instructions for a contest and announces the winners of an earlier puzzle.

The innovative games, puzzles, quizzes, and problems of this 40-page 8-by-10¾-inch bimonthly are capital. The bountiful potpourri of any issue will amuse and fascinate the young while stimulating the thinking processes. All ages of the range suggested by the publisher are served, with a few pages for the youngest and more for older children. The pages are meant to be pencil marked, and this makes some librarians qualmish; however, such an appealing magazine needs to be made known to children and their parents. Furthermore, adults brought up on these kinds of games (such as this writer) will need to be advised to resist the temptation of penciling in the answers, particularly when the subscription belongs to a child.

The Goldfinch
State Historical Society of Iowa
402 Iowa Ave., Iowa City, IA 52240
4 issues a year: September, November, February, and April
$10

Named for the state bird, this school-year quarterly presents "Iowa History for Young People"; the subscribers need not be citizens of the state to learn about it or to consider shared history. Each 32-page issue focuses on a theme; recent themes have included the family farm, Iowa folklife, forts, life on the prairie, regionalist art and literature, women's suffrage, and Iowa and World War I, this last theme an example of Iowa's involvement in national and world history. The intent is to help children imagine the long-ago by recreating earlier times through words and pictures and by relating events and activities to things children do and like today. The text is quite readable; consideration has been given to the reading abilities and interests of the intended audience, children ages 8 to 14. Black-and-white photographs accompany articles, but many lack clear definition because they are the work of early, unskilled photographers, a handicap for which there is no correction. Drawings and maps are presented with great clarity.

A map of Iowa usually appears in each issue, but the subject of the map varies (often related to the theme) from the number of family farms currently in every county, to upcoming folk festivals, to a challenging maze. Among other regular columns are "History Makers," calling for contributions about things children have discovered regarding Iowa history, which can be submitted in the form of verse, story, or artwork; and "History Mystery," an early photograph with a few clues in the adjacent paragraphs. "Disk Detective" offers a program to type into an IBM or Apple computer. Crossword puzzles, word matches, and spy codes are among the items that exercise the mind. Projects are suggested. Board games, songs, and verses add variety to the contents of the issues. Occasionally, there are instructions for a game played long ago.

The magazine is particularly noteworthy for its attempts to feature the many heritages of the state (including the contributions of Indians) and its coverage of women and of course children. Diaries, letters, remembrances, and other first-person accounts are used to good effect. Difficult words are explained and questions urge readers to think further about topics. The quarterly introduces social and political history and tries to help children gain an understanding of reliable sources for studying history. The goldfinch, in caricature, shows up now and then on the 7¾-by-8-inch pages. A single color is used on the cover and pages within to brighten the layout.

The Green Mountaineer
Vermont Historical Society
109 State St., Montpelier, VT 05602
3 issues a year: Fall, Winter, and Spring
$5

Published for the Vermont Junior Historian Program, this magazine is intended for sixth graders; however, teachers report using the 16-page, 8-by-8-inch magazine in grades four to seven. A few short, fully illustrated articles appear in an issue along with puzzles, activities, reports from subscribers, and regular columns. The focus, quite rightly, is on Vermont's history, but much of that story is significant to U.S. history too. One issue features skyscrapers in Vermont, including an article on Vermonter Otis (inventor of the safety elevator), and the border disputes over the Connecticut River. Another issue carries articles about sculpture, although it is not the publisher's intent to publish theme issues. Articles about the life and work of sculptor Larkin Mead are followed by one in which children are encouraged to make their own snow figures and another about sculpture in public places in Vermont.

Among the regularly appearing pieces are the letters to the editor with comments about the magazine, news from history clubs, and paragraphs from readers about things they have done relevant to Vermont history; and "It Happened On," a sentence or two about a half dozen events within the same months covered by the issue. "What's It?" asks subscribers to identify tools of long ago, and "History Hidden in the Paper World of Ephemera" presents the past as found in broadsheets, ads, paper labels and food packages, posters, greeting cards, and so forth.

The magazine makes good use of black-and-white photographs, drawings, and maps from the Vermont Historical Society and other archives in the state. The subject matter or focus of each illustration stands out clearly. A touch of a single color brightens the pages of every issue. The cover design and the layout of text and illustration within are inviting. Difficult words are printed in boldface and defined at the end of the article. An index is available covering the magazine's contents from the initial issue in Fall 1981 to Spring 1988.

Hidden Pictures Magazine
Highlights for Children, Inc.
Edit: 2300 W. Fifth Ave., P.O. Box 269, Columbus, OH 43216
Subs: P.O. Box 53781, Boulder, CO 80322
Bimonthly; $14.95

A bimonthly "from *Highlights*" for ages 6 to 10, each issue is chockful of puzzles. The challenge to find objects hidden in a picture begins on the cover where objects lie in wait in a touched-up color photograph. Within are hidden-picture puzzles of varying degrees of difficulty, from the "super challenge" of the centerfold to those with words hidden in the drawing. While almost half the pages carry a full-page hidden-picture illustration, other puzzles and amusements also fill the 34 colorful pages of the magazine.

In one issue, and most issues carry similar puzzles and pictorial matter, there are matching games, mazes and paths to follow, codes to decipher, counting and math calculations, mystery photographs, optical illusions, card and other tricks, simple science experiments, logic puzzles, riddles and jokes, puns, humorous verses, and of course the pictures in which to find the "unusual things." On the back cover appears "Brainstorm Brian's" various contraptions with their Rube Goldberg sequences.

The 8⅜-by-10⅞-inch pages all have some color on them, and many colors are used in an issue. Even the black-and-white drawings for the hidden pictures are framed in color. Although the magazine carries no articles or stories, it is certainly more cheerful than some of the workbook pages marketed for the home these days. Certainly perceptual skills will be put to use and sharpened.

Highlights for Children
Edit: 803 Church St., Honesdale, PA 18431
Subs: P.O. Box 269, Columbus, OH 43272
Monthly; except bimonthly July/August
$19.95

For many years "Fun with a Purpose" has appeared under the name-plate on this publication's cover. The magazine continues to present "wholesome fun" to help children grow "in basic skills and knowledge, in creativeness, in ability to think and reason, in sensitivity to others, in high ideals, and worthy ways of living." The monthly is intended for children of all ages, "from young listeners to independent readers," and carries stories, articles, and regular items appropriate to various reading and interest levels. The diversity of subject matter places this magazine among the few general-interest ones available for children. Offered in the 42 pages (50 in two issues) are fiction stories—some humorous, some exciting, and some about animals; nonfiction articles—about science, about famous people; crafts and projects; puzzles, hidden pictures, and word games; and contributions from children. Such a miscellany has characterized certain magazines meant to amuse and instruct children for over a century and *Highlights* for almost half a century. The annual index is in the December issue. Issues are designed to be enjoyed without writing on or destroying the pages.

The contents page typically lists about 30 entries. A graph on the right alerts parents and teachers to the content of each entry with regard to subject matter (the arts, science and nature, the nation and world) and reading level (preparation for reading, easy reading, more advanced reading). Dots on the graph also indicate items that contribute to "thinking and creating" and "moral values." The graph confirms the diversity of the content and an underlying tone. Free-lancers are advised that stories must "leave a good emotional and moral residue."

In the January 1990 issue, not unlike other issues, five two-page fiction stories are published. Two are classed as easy reading and the others as more advanced reading. All are light and humorous, and each bears an underlying but not overstated value. In "Jeffrey's Dragon," the stuffed animal has become dirty and in need of mending because of too much sharing at school, so Jeffrey's father (not his mother!) sews and washes the toy for him. A beginning reader would be able to handle the story because there are so many monosyllabic words, and those with two syllables (and the very few with three) are frequently repeated. Only slightly more difficult to read is "The Princess and the Star" about a long-ago young royal with an affinity for stars who settles for the ones always found in the cross-section of an apple. Smaller typeface, along with more words to a page, characterize the print of the stories for more advanced readers. A mysterious visitor uncovers "A Secret at Finley House." The story also offers, according to the editor, "an insight into understanding and communication between two generations." The Ickirag and other critters are the source of "Mr. McMuddle's Troubles," but a thorough cleaning of his unkempt house sends these inhabitants running. In "Percival, the Pizza-Eating Penguin," the aroma turns out to be better than the taste.

An equal number of nonfiction articles regularly appears. In the same issue are five, all for more advanced readers. Two fall into the science-and-nature category. In a first-person account, the author invites readers to join a "Night Hike: Peeking at Possums in Australia"; seven color photographs help establish the scene. Another evening venture, far flung too, is titled "Visible Venus"; the article gives short descriptions of the planet's winter appearance and two columns of instructions for tracking Venus for several months in the evening sky. Two articles are biographical. "Log Cabin Composer" profiles Edward MacDowell and adds a simple piano arrangement of "To a Wild Rose." In "Billy Mills: Olympic Lightning," the exciting finish of a race makes for drama. The author injects, "His victory had shown that anything is possible with hard work and determination." The fifth article, "A Last Look at the Amazon Jungle," is about vanishing rain forests. The nonfiction articles, as well as the fiction stories, are generally two pages in length, seldom longer.

Among the beginning pages, a poem is usually set within a full-page and fitting illustration. The work of the finest living children's poets is often showcased. The page is particularly worthy of praise. While a poetry book loses some value by being heavily illustrated, the framework here seems to say that poetry is important.

As many as 15 (or half) of the contents page entries are for regularly published items a page or less in length. Some appear in practically every issue, and some have been around for years. "Hidden Pictures" has challenged the visual acuity of more than one generation of children. In "Goofus and Gallant," the bad boy and the good boy (the best and worst of behavior) are pictured. The wooden Timbertoes, Tommy and Mabel, cavort monthly within a dozen picture frames, their playfulness described in an easy vocabulary under the line drawings. The young mind is put to work in "Thinking" where diverse questions, a few open ended, are posed along with pictorial matter and in "Headwork" where progressively more difficult questions are asked and children are instructed to "see how far you can go, thinking of good answers from your own head." Reading skills are exercised in "Matching," two sets of simple pictures to link, and "Fun with Phonics," where pictures are also used to elicit verbal responses. "Things to Make," one of the magazine's finer features, describes projects that are not only clever and simple but can usually be readily made from materials at hand with minimal instructions. Frequently, the suggestion is made that someone might enjoy receiving the end product as a gift. "For Wee Folks" is a special page of assorted challenges dealing with counting, ordering, naming, discriminating, and so forth. (Do children of this age object to being called "wee"?) Within "Riddles and Jokes" are a few exchanges that seem a little threadbare, but the punchlines are probably new to young readers.

Children are encouraged to contribute to the magazine and do so. In the letters to the editor are comments about the magazine and questions about social and emotional concerns of the correspondents. "Our Own Pages" is a double-page spread of poems and drawings by subscribers. Occasionally, there are special calls for particular artwork or writing from children.

The busy front cover for many, many years has announced the "fun" of the magazine. Jolly, active children (and merry adults or animals) seemingly move about the cover; the eye can hardly keep up with them. The back cover, in a way, spoofs the front. "What's Wrong?" allows for innumerable corrections and could even prompt some imaginative possibilities beyond the expected. An October issue shows a swingin' barn dance on the front cover and the crazy refreshment stand at the shindig on the back. Children are asked to count how many things they find wrong on the back cover. Maybe they could also think about which mistake is the most outlandish.

The monthly is and always has been highly pictorial. Variety is evident in the illustrations. Color photographs, cartoons, drawings, and sketches are found between the covers of any issue. Every page is in color. Five out of six pages show many colors; on the others, a single color is used for borders or backgrounds. The layout is busy, as intended, but not overly so. Typefaces are clear and legible.

The monthly seeks to satisfy a wide range of ages (2 to 12) and readers (remedial to gifted), and for this reason, there will always be some content not of interest to a particular reader. Nevertheless, the magazine has its appeal, and some features and editorial perspectives are embraced by many folks. Certainly, fostering "wholesome human relations" is a worthy aim. Those looking for an alternative to certain print and video materials marketed for children will appreciate that "violence is taboo" in *Highlights*.   *Children's Magazine Guide*

Hopscotch
P.O. Box 1292, Saratoga Springs, NY 12866
Bimonthly; $13.50

Started in 1989, "The Magazine for Young Girls" targets those between 8 and 10 years of age but hopes to serve the range from 6 to 12. The emphasis of the bimonthly is on activities and hobbies (leaving human sexuality, cosmetics, and fashion to other magazines). Each 40-page issue usually carries three nonfiction articles; a story or two; some verses; and a few puzzles, crafts, or recipes. The full-color cover of the 7-by-9-inch magazine often pictures a winsome lass the age of the intended audience. Semiglossy paper is used within. A single color is used in each issue to highlight and decorate captions and drawings. Black-and-white snapshots are reproduced on a few pages. Ample white space is allowed on the pages, including space around the letters of the typeface.

Not that issues have themes, but usually three or so of the articles are linked by subject to the cover. A dozen teddy bears bunched together on one cover hint of articles within about two girls who collect them, a factory that produces over 40 models, and the origin and popularity of the toy. A photograph, presumably taken in the People's Republic of China, introduces a story about the life of a typical young girl of Shanghai, information about Chinese New Year celebrations, and instructions for holding chopsticks, along with a recipe for which they can be used. Another issue announces on the cover "Looking Back to Yesterday." The lead article is about Civil War times; the other long piece is about two girls who traced their family history. A one-page item summarizes Alex Haley's investigations for *Roots*. Articles generally run four to seven pages in length and try to approach the subjects from a young girl's point of view.

Fictional stories are sometimes seasonal, other times folktales. One story centers on friendship. Several short verses are usually printed in an issue, some on a poetry page. The verse is apparently from free-lancers. One issue features a nine-page narrative about a Schnauzer who has "twenty-nine different sweaters and jackets" from which to chose and who takes a liking to Silver Lady.

Among items boxed in the bottom right corner of the contents page are references to short nonfiction pieces that focus on animals—marsupials, turtles, skunks, and those pieces that might examine pets or pumpkins. These are usually captioned "Science" or "Nature." Occasionally, there are word puzzles or pages to color. Some issues offer instructions for making simple craft items and cookies, while another issue outlines steps for planning a party. Worthwhile books that relate to the subjects of the issue are suggested. At the very end of the magazine is "Potsy's P.O." where the letters to the magazine are published. Potsy is a rabbit that hops about every issue. "Insiders" at the front gives brief information about the authors and illustrators.

Humpty Dumpty's Magazine
Children's Better Health Institute
Edit: Benjamin Franklin Literary & Medical Society, Inc., 1100
    Waterway Blvd., P.O. Box 567, Indianapolis, IN 46206
Subs: P.O. Box 7133, Red Oak, IA 51591
Monthly; except bimonthly January–August (8 issues)
$11.95

This health-oriented magazine for children ages four to six is packed with stories, poems, and activities, often (but not always) with an underlying message about good health, nutrition, exercise, and hygiene. Humpty appears on each cover and tries to make the reader laugh about his cleverness, or lack of cleverness, in "Humpty at Home," a regular two-page cartoon. Occasionally, Humpty surprises the reader by being revealed in a dot-to-dot puzzle. His silhouette, a seated egg with white collar and crossed legs, ends each longer piece. Its table of contents divided into "Health Pages" and "More Fun," the 48-page magazine seeks to offer variety within. Stories captioned "More Fun" often rely on the health-and-good-habits slant of the magazine and come down firmly on this emphasis.

A typical issue brings a poem or an activity to the left of the table of contents followed by a five- to six-page story dealing with problems encountered by young children, such as nighttime fears. In a recent issue, "Old Tatters," Katie's favorite blanket, serves a new purpose as she finds a way to be less dependent on it. Some of the material acquaints preschoolers with shapes, weather, seasons, and holidays, along with the emphasis on health. Among the regularly appearing puzzles are hidden pictures and dot-to-dot pages. Most issues present a recipe a child can make with adult supervision. Each issue includes "Get Cozy with a Book," a book review for children that shows the book cover; "You Draw the Pictures," from subscribers; "Your Body Machine," factual information about the human body (focusing on elbows, hiccups, and the like); and "Ask Dr. Cory," a medical column of questions from parents answered by the doctor.

Illustrations vary from simple black-and-white line drawings and cartoons to brightly colored pictures. Full-color photographs are rarely used, and thus the child's never-never land comes through in the exaggerations of the characteristics (human and animal) of many illustrations. And yet there are the contrasting soft touches between the covers of every issue. The pictorial matter and numerous games and activities are the hallmarks of this 6½-by-9⅛-inch magazine. The variety of amusements is remarkable: things to make and paper-folding projects; mazes and rebus stories; counting this and that; thinking of the right words; finding similarities and noting differences; and the ever-alluring what's-wrong-with-this-picture puzzle.

The stories are generally humorous with a bit of suspense. Beginning readers might tackle some of the tales, especially those for which vocabulary clues are provided in the illustrations. This magazine is very much like others for young ones by this publisher; *Turtle* and *Children's Playmate* overlap with *Humpty Dumpty* with regard to ages of targeted audience.   *Children's Magazine Guide*

Illinois History
Illinois Historic Preservation Agency
Old State Capitol, Springfield, IL 62701
Monthly during school year: October–May (8 issues)
$8

Intended primarily for secondary schools in one state, this monthly, published in cooperation with the Illinois State Historical Society, serves as an example of the type of periodical that might be encouraged in any state. All the articles in an issue, with the exception of the introductory one, are written by students in grades 7 through 12. The contributions represent some of the finest nonfiction writing by youths. Perhaps in the prepublication processes, teachers and editors are attentively guiding and directing the efforts. Maybe brevity is the criterion that prompts clear, crisp prose. Whatever, the articles consistently offer informative and pleasurable reading, an accomplishment that should not go unnoticed.

Each issue centers on a theme and is introduced in a feature essay by an expert in the field. A list of suggested readings is boxed at the end of the essay. An average of 10 articles follow, each usually two pages in length, occasionally three or one. The investigations of the students are complemented by illustrations from the Illinois State Historical Library and sometimes a few other sources. Black-and-white photographs and drawings are used generously on the 20 pages of an issue; maps and portraits are added when appropriate. Sources are briefly cited at the end of each article. Authors are identified by name, school, and school location.

Among the themes for issues of one recent school year are "The Interplay of Illinois' Rivers and Its Culture," "Illinois and the Great Migration," "Domestic Interior Furnishings in Nineteenth- and Twentieth-Century Illinois," "Transformation of Women's Labor in Illinois," and "Community History." The February issue always pays tribute to Lincoln. On the back cover are listed upcoming themes along with a paragraph of statements and questions to trigger the thinking of contributors. The suggestions attest to the abundance of possibilities for developing the themes and hint of the variety of topics within any given issue. The May issue carries an index for the year.

The emphasis of the content is, with just reason, on the historical, but the past is related to the present and the near past, thus helping the young see the significance of events that happened before their birth. The periodical lives up to its subtitle "A Magazine for Young People."

Illinois is a state of such diversity, even opposites, that material on the subjects of some issues might well be requested in school and public libraries outside the state. Where common interests prevail, the magazine is likely to be useful. Families that travel in Illinois might want home subscriptions. Two subscriptions are sent free on request to all schools in Illinois.

Jack and Jill
Children's Better Health Institute
Edit: Benjamin Franklin Literary & Medical Society, Inc., 1100
    Waterway Blvd., P.O. Box 567, Indianapolis, IN 46206
Subs: P.O. Box 7133, Red Oak, IA 51591
Monthly; except bimonthly January–August (8 issues)
$11.95

The targeted age range for this magazine has recently been upped to 7 through 10, still overlapping with *Children's Playmate* at the lower end and *Child Life* at the top of the range. As with the other five titles from this publisher, the emphasis is on health. Great variety is evident in the text and illustrations within an issue. Fiction is usually humorous, the work of free-lancers. Puzzles and games, as well as crafts and activities, are a regular part of the content. Children are urged to make contributions to a few of the 48 pages of an issue. On about two-thirds of the pages, several colors are used; others are without color. The cover of the 6½-by-9⅛-inch magazine is in full color, often a drawing, sometimes a photograph.

Typically, about a half dozen stories and articles appear in an issue with the weight in terms of number and length usually in favor of fiction. Although health and seasonal subjects are not wanting, many of the pieces are about animals. Those with a slant on health are listed on the contents page under "Health Features"; the others, under "More Fun." Recipes too are usually mentioned under "Health Features," as is the health-advice column, "Ask Dr. Cory." Entries on the contents page listed under "From Our Readers" include "Jokes and Riddles," "Poetry by Our Readers," and "Picture Exhibition," consisting of line drawings.

Among the regular "Special Features" of the contents page are "Jack and Jill's World Marathon," a color comic strip in which the two youngsters rocket to other times and places, and "Jack and Jill's Snapshot Album," a few facts and some drawings about things they've seen on their excursions. Members of a cast of nine characters, "Mirthworms," appear variously in a black-and-white simply drawn cartoonlike strip. The other items listed in this section of the contents page, in issues examined, number from three to eight and make up the word play, matching games, crossword puzzles, mazes, hidden and dot-to-dot pictures, and other games and puzzles long associated with the magazine. These tend to take seasonal subjects for their focus.

The layout of the pages is much like that of the other magazines for younger children from the Institute. Differences can be noted in the greater amount of text and the occasional use of photographs for illustration. Other illustrations show the diversity typical of the publisher, with a leaning toward line drawings. Many of the illustrators seem to be cartoonists.

Jack and Jill is made available by the Library of Congress in braille and on audio disc recording. *Children's Magazine Guide*

Junior Scholastic
Scholastic Inc.
Edit: 730 Broadway, New York, NY 10003
Subs: 2931 E. McCarty St., P.O. Box 3710, Jefferson City, MO 65102
Biweekly during school year (18 issues)
$8; $5.25 each for 10 or more subscriptions to same address

Published continuously since 1937, this social studies and current events magazine for grades six to eight helps junior high readers keep up with the news and delve into this country's history through the articles and illustrations of this biweekly classroom periodical. A year-long map and map skills program is tied to the articles and shorter pieces. An issue usually runs to 16 or 24 pages; center inserts might be included. Advertisements are carried at the front and back.

Captions used rather consistently to categorize articles on the contents page are "U.S. History," "U.S. Geography," "Nation," and "World." Regular items, placed toward the end of an issue, include various skills exercises and quizzes, crossword puzzles, and "Currents," a page of brief news items. In issues reviewed, the U.S. history sections examine the westward movement after the Civil War and provide the script for a play about Nat Turner's rebellion. Under U.S. geography, the focus of the two-page spread is a state or part of the country, for example, Alaska or the northern plains. A map in color shows the area; clear, full-color photographs depict certain facets of life there; and commentary is made about the area's current scene and the possible prospects and problems of the future. World news discusses the Berlin Wall and follows up the cover photograph with a study of Indonesia. In one issue, the subject under "Nation" is children and guns (contents page questions offer much to consider) and in another, the Supreme Court. Following a very readable article, four actual cases are briefly presented for students to debate. The Court's decisions are printed at the back of the issue.

One issue carries two features that would be handy to keep. One is about the census—the what, why, and how—as well as the history of taking the census and how the information gained from the population count might be used. The other feature gives brief biographical information and black-and-white photographs of leaders in the executive, legislative, and judicial branches of the U.S. government. The same issue presents two valuable charts about the states, giving origins of their names, capitals, governors, and so forth in cne and statistical information—poverty rate, violent crimes, per capita income, and several population categories, for example—in the other.

The magazine prints many photographs. Full color is used on most pages; touches of color are added to the rest. The layout is attractive and uncluttered. The eye is drawn to the page and easily moves around it to pick up the illustrative and highlighted matter before biting into the article. The highly pictorial front cover gives evidence of careful thought with regard to lettering, photographs, and placement.

Although the exercises peg this as a classroom magazine, the biweekly is informative, and the writing is solid and straightforward. An individual subscription could help make both U.S. history and current events significant to a young person, particularly the one who wants or needs something other than textbooks or the accounts of national newspapers.

Children's Magazine Guide

Kid City
> **Children's Television Workshop**
> Edit: One Lincoln Plaza, New York, NY 10023
> Subs: P.O. Box 53349, Boulder, CO 80322
> Monthly; except February and August (10 issues)
> $13.97

Formerly *Electric Company Magazine*, this lively monthly is intended "for graduates of *Sesame Street*," children 6 to 10. The table of contents lists some 15 items; types of features (stories, regularly appearing sections) are not indicated in the listing, but a colored square to the left of a title codes the areas of interest, primarily curricular. The monthly seldom extends its pictorial stories beyond three pages. Every issue is amusing and humorous yet carries a goodly amount of fascinating information and sufficiently challenging material. Color and variety abound in this magazine that is at once playful and educational. The smiling children of the full-color cover photographs usually signal that there is fun within and pictorially announce the issue's theme.

Among subjects used recently as issue themes are pets, bats, eyes, and archaeology. Each issue generally brings a two-page nonfiction piece and an equally long fiction story. The initial feature as of late has been a two-page spread of several close-up color photographs of members of the animal kingdom (for example, reindeer) or parts of their bodies (nose). The photographs are in keeping with the issue's theme. In an issue about pets, the winning stories and snapshots (pet *and* child) extend to three pages. This same issue features an appealing photo story about a boy whose family runs a llama ranch in Colorado. A few other features of the issue about pets merit mentioning because they are representative of material published in the magazine. A multiple-choice quiz checks on things children need to know about taking care of pets. Another two-page feature tells how to prepare food and nesting material for wild birds. "The Story of Balto" is presented as a comic strip, although lines at the bottom of the page note that it is a true story of a famous sled dog.

An issue's puzzles and activities are typical of those found in children's magazines of other publishers, but the imaginative touches here make the games superior to most. In a survey, subscribers chose five favorite activities: mazes (most favored), hidden pictures, word hunts, "What's Wrong with This Picture?" and "Make Your Own Cartoon." In the issue about pets, the maze requires a pet gerbil to travel transparent red tubes to get to his dinner. The birds of the hidden-picture puzzle are not concealed in the drawing but in their natural habitat; a checklist names the 10 birds to find (black-capped chickadee, for example). In the cartoon contest, children are to supply the dialogue for the balloons; four of the winners are published in a subsequent issue. The humor is delightful, far from strained.

Among the features appearing fairly regularly are "True But Strange," odd trivia often related to the issue's theme, and "Kid City News," brief reports about children across the country and some book recommendations. "Pencil Power" puzzles include rebus messages, matching items, and finding words. In "Tickle Yourself," readers' favorite jokes are published in a fully illustrated, colorful double-page spread. The repartee is printed in balloons, and the speakers are shown in caricature. (Joke pages in other magazines are certainly bland by comparison.) Near the end of each issue is "Photo Finish," a spectacular shot—a peacock, snow surfing, a stuffed animal drying on a clothesline—with a paragraph of explanation that also points out elements to be observed in the full-color photograph. "Poet's Corner" often presents submissions from subscribers but occasionally prints the work of a respected contemporary poet for children.

Most of the 32 pages (plus covers) of this $8\frac{1}{8}$-by-$10\frac{3}{4}$-inch magazine are filled with fine fare for the young. The color code on the contents page places each article, game, or activity into one or two subject areas: art, math, language, reading, science, social studies, history, or sport. Seemingly, the most frequently used categories are reading and science. The full-color monthly gives a freshness to its content and format that can nourish inquisitive children and continue to make learning pleasurable for them.

Kid City carries ads. In a recent issue, six pages (one-sixth of those available) are full-page advertisements; two pages for a cereal, in the form of a cartoon, cannot be readily distinguished from the content prepared by the editorial offices.   *Children's Magazine Guide*

KidSports
ProServ, Inc.
1101 Wilson Blvd., Arlington, VA 22209
Quarterly; $6

A new entry in a territory where upstarts have not fared well, this quarterly has the backing of a sports marketing and management company. The publisher notes that in almost every article the importance of practice is stressed. The advice is usually from professional athletes. Another intent is to offer inspirational pieces, in part to counter negative press some players have received for drugs and crime. Intended for ages 8 to 14, the 32-page full-color magazine sorts its material on the contents page under "Features," "Instruction," and "Departments."

In the most recent issue available for inspection, one of the features is about the winning performances of a soccer goalkeeper, now on the U.S. team. Another is a two-page piece about skateboarding, with one page a full-color photograph of a skateboarder (in the air, of course). The third feature is a five-page fiction story about the preseason practice of a high school basketball team. "Anthony's Challenge" is about an enigmatic black but superb player on a white team.

The "Instruction" articles, for which players are given authorship, are (in this issue) by Larry Bird, Mary Lou Retton, and Wayne Gretzky. "The FUNdamentals of Practice" and "When I Was Your Age" suggest the tenor of the articles in this issue, as well as earlier issues. These articles are often longer than the items named under "Features." Under "Departments" are listed the puzzles and posters. The centerfold in the latest issue pulls out to offer color photographs of two of the "instructors" of the issue. Other departments use as a promotional character Punchy of Hawaiian Punch, a sponsor of the magazine that is also represented in the ads. About one-fourth of the pages carry advertisements.

Under the nameplate is the line, "The Official Sports Magazine for Kids," but the reason for the designation "official" could not be ascertained. The full-color photographs of well-known athletes on the 8⅜-by-10⅞-inch, glossy-coated pages will appeal to many youngsters. Many children will not mind being encouraged to take their practice seriously.

Know Your World Extra
Field Publications
Edit: 245 Long Hill Rd., Middletown, CT 06457
Subs: 4343 Equity Dr., Columbus, OH 43228
Biweekly during school year (18 issues)
$13.98; $6.99 each for 10 or more subscriptions to same address
Intended for students in grades 6 through 12 having difficulty with school subjects, this classroom periodical is written, according to the publisher, at second- and third-grade reading levels. As with the other newsmagazines from Field, a pictorial front page introduces a major article. Inside, the top of a page typically carries a caption in small print and an oversized headline. Most of the captions are the same as in the periodicals for students reading at grade level: "News Feature," "News Short," and "Science." "Daily Living" offers help with fractions, reading want ads, and preventing accidents, among other things. The center four pages usually carry a story, often a true one. The puzzle of an issue's back page frequently works on developing vocabulary.

Cover stories in recent issues focus on an earthquake, race relations, and waste disposal problems. The stories are suitably developed despite the constraints of a limited word list. The shorter reports tend to be about teenagers overcoming problems and sports-related topics. In issues examined, a young person in a photograph is more likely to be male than female.

Drawings and black-and-white photographs share space almost equally with text on the 8⅛-by-11⅜-inch pages. Touches of color are added here and there in each biweekly issue. The 12-page newsprint magazine seeks to satisfy junior and senior high students who would not be able to handle the vocabulary in other newsmagazines prepared by Field Publications. Supplementary material is furnished the classroom teacher in the form of a book of spirit duplicating masters.

Koala Club News
Zoological Society of San Diego, Inc.
Edit: P.O. Box 551, San Diego, CA 92112
Subs: San Diego Zoo Membership, P.O. Box 271, San Diego, CA
   92112
Quarterly; $9

The emphasis of this eight-page quarterly is on the animals of the San Diego Zoo and Wild Animal Park and the activities of its widely traveled staff. In issues examined, one or two major articles are printed on the 10-by-14-inch pages, along with "Critters of the Quarter." The writing is straightforward and the pieces informative. Almost half the space is given over to black-and-white photographs of inhabitants of the zoo and park or animals in their natural habitats. In two issues, the cover stories (and therefore most of the issues) are about the "wilds of Africa" and Tiger River, a new area of the zoo representing a tropical rain forest. The regular feature about a "critter" has depicted the porcupine, yellow-billed hornbill, and Sumatran tiger. The full-page stunning black-and-white photograph of the animal kingdom member is framed by a border, making it suitable for hanging. "Crafty's Corner" suggests projects for children; a busy beaver saws away in the pictorial heading. The issues formerly carried children's contributions in "Porky Pine's Pen Pals" and a page for coloring (and the editorial profile indicates that these features are continued); however, they do not appear in issues sent for examination.

The articles can be read without much difficulty by those above the beginning-to-read level. The layout is particularly attractive, allowing the reader or viewer to concentrate on the text or illustration. Decorative touches are kept light and lively. The masthead supports a koala at a type-writer. A single color brightens each issue; the color changes from issue to issue.

The publication is intended for age 15 and under and is obtained through membership in the Koala Club, which includes unlimited admission to the zoo and park for the year and some special passes. Although this hints of advantages to those living near San Diego, the quarterly could be appreciated by children (and adults) in homes and libraries where there is an interest in animals, zoos, and conservation.

Ladybug
Carus Corp.
Edit: 315 Fifth St., Peru, IL 61354
Subs: P.O. Box 58342, Boulder, CO 80322
Monthly; $24.97

Because this monthly is scheduled for publication in September 1990, this description must be based solely on a review copy of the premier issue. From the publisher of *Cricket* comes *Ladybug*, "the magazine for young children." Intended for ages two to seven, the 8-by-9¼-inch monthly uses color and particularly legible typeface on all pages. In keeping with the other magazine, this one too plans to present the very finest in story and illustration in its three dozen pages.

Among the content to appear regularly are two sets of characters and a story to be read to the child. In the first issue, "The Naughty Shoes" is an eight-page fantasy about the nighttime adventures and daytime mix-ups of many different pairs of shoes. The story is by Dutch author Paul Biegel (translated by Cilia Amidon) and illustrated by Victoria Chess. As for the regular characters, "Tom and Pippo" by Helen Oxenbury tells of an incident in the lives of a toddler and his father in a four-page, four-picture story using simple language. "Matt and Big Dog" relates the joyful excursions and special delights of a young fellow and his large pet. Presented in a form similar to a comic strip with several pictures on a page, the sensitively drawn family and friends and the tender story are far from being cartoonlike.

Poetry certainly will appear regularly. The initial issue contains "I Want to Meet" (Ladybug and her family) by David McCord with illustration by Hilary Knight. Mother Goose is represented by "Cock-a-doodle doo" and the handsome rooster of Arnold Lobel. An informative piece about "the world around us" will explore familiar places; the zoo, circus, supermarket, and airport are on the proposed itineraries. The first visit is to a house being built. Two double-page spreads picture how the work is coming along. Anthropomorphic workers busily pursue their occupations; their jobs, implements, and materials are identified by name.

The premier issue features "Twinkle, Twinkle, Little Star" with musical notations; other songs are promised. The frolicking children from the palette of Karen Gundersheimer interpret the body manipulations required of "Can You Do This?" On the back cover is a four-frame story of "Molly and Emmett," a girl and her cat. "Bees and Bugs," a two-page test of visual discrimination, shows larger-than-life yellow-striped bees and huge domino-back ladybugs. A pull-out section to be cut up requires the matching of shoes (and thereby is related to the issue's read-aloud story). Other tasks slated for future issues involve matching colors and shapes; connecting, identifying, and classifying objects; and finding numbers and letters.

The quality of content, pictorial and verbal, and the quality of reproduction, particularly of the four-color illustrations (on semiglossy, sturdy paper), suggest that editor Marianne Carus will succeed in adding an exceptional title to her repertoire. The monthly is meant to be shared between parent and child; both should be delighted for their own reasons. The love of reading and joy of learning are promoted here.

Let's Find Out see *Scholastic Let's Find Out*

Math Magazine see *Scholastic Math Magazine*

Mazputniņš
    100 Cherry Hill Dr., Kalamazoo, MI 49007
    Monthly; $28
Published in Latvian, *Mazputniņš* (meaning "little bird") brings 32 pages of stories and puzzles for children through age 12. Although the circulation

is small and the target audience limited, it is of interest that the magazine also goes to Latvia and other parts of the world. The 8⅜-by-11-inch monthly is edited by volunteers and sponsored by the Latvian Institute. For children unfamiliar with the language, the magazine offers a chance to consider a non-English-language publication. Some of the pictorial matter needs no translation.

The variety in content is evident in even the size of typeface, for it can be noted a very large print is used for brief stories and poems for young children. Fiction in smaller print is probably for older children. Humorous and thoughtful stories and poems are included, as well as folktales. Usually, a few pages are devoted to science, particularly nature studies. Although puzzles are found in various parts of an issue, toward the end, several puzzle pages are captioned "Mini manu minamo!" Mazes, crossword puzzles, dot-to-dot pictures, matching of items, and math problems are meant to challenge. Instructions for activities requiring paper folding or cutout patterns are provided on the pullout centerfold of heavy stock. Jokes and contributions from subscribers, as well as a song inside the back cover, round out an issue.

Illustrations are primarily line drawings. A few decorative pieces, mostly humorous, sometimes informative, set the tone for stories. Touches of color are sparingly used in some issues; typically, a few color sheets are inserted. Some pages could probably be colored by subscribers.

Merlyn's Pen
> P.O. Box 1058, East Greenwich, RI 02818
> 4 issues during school year: October/November, December/January, February/March, and April/May
> $14.95; $7.95 each for 11 to 20 subscriptions to same address; $7.95 each for 21 or more

Next to the attractive lettering of the cover's nameplate are the words "The National Magazine of Student Writing." Intended for grades 7 to 10, this first-rate literary magazine seeks to provide a niche for writers who are too old to contribute to children's magazines and too young to enter the territory open to high school juniors and seniors. The styles of writing are appropriately diverse. Every issue brings fiction, poetry, and essays that are quite engaging and would be appreciated beyond the specified grade-level range for submissions. The main appeal for junior high readers should be the opportunity to taste of some of the best writing by peers.

The submissions focus on concerns that are real and pressing in our society and obviously of interest and import to many young people. The editors deserve kudos for creating a vehicle for thoughtful adolescent writers and for nurturing their efforts. Contributors are urged to send manuscripts that "grip the readers' interest and stir the heart or mind." The published works generally succeed in doing so. Although a serious and even somber tone permeates many of the offerings, the stories ring true, and the expressive and honest writing affords rewarding reading experiences. Inasmuch as some adults work through their anxieties by writing, why not allow the young the same catharsis? Even so, "the customary topics of family, personal, and peer conflict," to name a few, are offset by the humor of some of the shorter pieces, poems, and illustrations.

Accepted submissions are grouped on the contents page under "Features," "Pen and Stars," and "Departments." The last brings comments from the editor (or guest) in "Notes from the Cave" and responses from readers about writing in previous issues in "Afterwords." Other reactions to earlier stories and poems are published in "Letters to the Pen," along with letters in praise of the magazine and calls for support of action groups (against animal exploitation, for example). "Syntactic Conundrums" presents challenges, and "Syntactic Solutions" presents the answers to these challenges. For two other items under the department category—"Shorts" and "Reviews and Retrospects"—page numbers are given, but the specific submissions and their authors are specified in other parts of the contents page.

Under "Features" are listed a dozen or so contributions, giving for each title, author, and type of piece. Most entries are labeled story or poem; other tags used are essay, review, humor, parable, and haiku. The magazine accepts science fiction and nonfiction; however, few stories are of these genres. Poems are also recorded under "Pen and Stars," where as many as 10 are listed in issues examined. It is the case that two poems printed on the same page within can be placed in different sections of the contents page. The distinguishing factor is not evident; perhaps it is an editorial judgment of quality. Generally, four items under "Pen and Stars" are not poetry; they are usually submissions about a half page in length. The magazine also accepts plays; parodies; book and movie reviews; and drawings, cartoons, and other artwork.

The contributors must be in grades 7 to 10, although some of their work is published after they have moved on. For each story there is always a paragraph telling about the author's interests and when the story was written. At the end of many stories is a note from the author about his or her writing of the piece. Only 2 to 3 percent of the work read by the editorial staff is published. Every submission is read by at least two editors, and each contributor receives a decision letter and brief comment within 11 weeks. R. Jim Stahl heads a stable of about 15 editors. He created this fine magazine and undoubtedly should be credited for maintaining its quality—and respecting the abilities of young writers.

The full-color cover illustrations of this 35-page school year quarterly are also the work of junior high students. Over the period of a year, the covers also hint of the diversity within. The uncluttered layout of the pages and the well-chosen typefaces underscore the regard for the writers' and illustrators' work. A four-page brochure, "The Activity Guide," is available to classroom teachers.

While this magazine is intended for children in two of the grade levels within this book's scope (seven and eight), some avid readers in lower grades will find the reading matter both interesting and challenging. The editors caution, however, that there are stories of child abuse and teen suicide. Be that as it may, the young authors undoubtedly speak more convincingly and forcefully than many of the didactic adult writers.

Classroom teachers have used the magazine with reported success. Librarians can offer *Merlyn's Pen* on their shelves. Parents and youth advocates might well find the content to be unparalleled for giving insight into the joys and frustrations of the young. For children and adults, the reading is choice, the writing imaginative.

Mickey Mouse Magazine
Welsh Publishing Group, Inc.
Edit: 300 Madison Ave., New York, NY 10017
Subs: P.O. Box 10598, Des Moines, IA 50340
Quarterly; $7.80

Unlike other Welsh magazines, this one intended for preschool children devotes nearly half its pages to parents in the section titled "Guide for Grown-ups: Ideas for Family Fun." The front portion of the quarterly is for the young ones. Mickey is usually shown on the cover; sometimes Minnie, Goofy, or other Disney pals join him. Ten or so items are listed on the contents page. Two are regularly appearing pieces: "Mickey Mail," with artwork and brief letters from the young audience, and "Goofy's Giggles," with jokes, seemingly solicited from readers across the country. About 20 of the 40 pages are intended for children ages two to six (an ad indicates three to eight). These pages are not interrupted by ads save for the one inside the front cover. In the part for adults, ads appear on every other page.

The section for children is colorful and highly pictorial. Illustrations are kept relatively simple. Many pages carry puzzles and activities; children may develop skills with numbers and letters, work through simple cross-word puzzles and mazes, follow instructions about coloring or drawing, read a rebus story, and find hidden pictures. Most of these items are a page or two in length as are the other features except for the humorous "read-together story" that usually runs to four pages. Minnie takes a leading role in a set of color photographs, on which her image is superimposed, about a party or some other form of amusement. Another fairly regular feature, not unexpectedly, is a two-page comic-strip story. Appropriately, some of the material is seasonal. Children will have fun with their lively half of this magazine published since 1988.

Misha
Soviet Union Magazine
Edit: 8 Ulitsa Moskvina, Moscow, 103772, USSR
Subs: Imported Publications, 320 W. Ohio St., Chicago, IL 60610
Monthly; $20

Published in the Soviet Union for export, the content of this monthly in English offers much variety. Issues typically include fiction stories, folk-tales, articles about science, verses and songs, things to do and make, rid-dles, and puzzles. Drawings of the Mishas, a smiling boy and teddy bear, bracket the title on the front cover. The various interest and reading levels make at least parts of every issue appropriate for children ages 6 to 12, although the publisher does not specify age levels. The illustrations, in general, are not particularly distinguished, and unevenness is evident in the writing. The magazine is printed on glossy paper of a suitable weight. The use of color in all 32 pages and the lively movement of some layouts are likely to entice some children.

In a recent issue, a half dozen heavily illustrated stories appear between the covers. The garish cover picturing a cartoon-like Baba-Yaga leads to a somewhat preposterous story about anthropomorphic mushrooms and the witch. For two humorous folktales, one from the Near East, the other from Vietnam, the pictorial matter shows some improvement; the texts read easily enough, and the problems of translation have been overcome. A Jules Verne story is retold in three pages, equally divided between text and illustration. A magical tale about Venice is accompanied by three reproductions of paintings by Italian illustrators of children's books. In a nonfiction article about the sunflower, history and nature are combined.

Contributions by children in one issue include a story written by two children about their grandparents, and two pages of letters and pictures from children around the world. Puzzles and games have some similarities to those found in many children's magazines. Suggestions for play range from hopscotch to chess moves. Instructions for making a string-puppet ostrich are probably sparse for an initial attempt. A story puppet that uses Russian words is adjacent to a report from Misha's information desk about the many languages of the world.

While the verse of one monthly issue most likely suffers from translation, in the same issue, the centerfold full-color photograph of sea gulls is exquisite. Typical of the middle range of text and illustration is the two-page cartoon about Wolf and Hare, who must have cousins in Disney's world.

The colorful breezy pictures of this "children's illustrated monthly" will appeal to a number of children. A noteworthy feature of the magazine is the publishing of the artwork of children from around the world. If one thinks it worthwhile to introduce children to a magazine from the Soviet Union, *Misha* would be a suitable choice. The title is also published in French, German, Spanish, Russian, Hungarian, Italian, and Mongolian. For information, write to Imported Publications.

My Weekly Reader see *Weekly Reader*

National Geographic World
National Geographic Society
Edit: 17th and M Sts., N.W., Washington, DC 20036
Subs: P.O. Box 2330, Washington, DC 20077
Monthly; $10.95

The Society's publication for children 8 to 13 aims to combine information and entertainment in factual stories and colorful pictures about people and places, science, sports, adventure, and animals. From three to five articles, in which illustrations dominate, are presented in issues of 32 pages, sometimes more. The full-color pictures on glossy-coated paper are in keeping with the well-known parent publication; however, page size is larger here, 8½ by 10¾ inches. Photographs in vivid color, obviously the products of skilled photographers, are found on every page, often filling a page and sometimes becoming a double-page spread. One- and two-page pieces, along with regular items, round out an issue.

The subject matter of this splendid and enlightening pictorial magazine is in keeping with the many interests of children. The articles are usually at least three pages in length and frequently six. Authors' names are not attached to articles, but a complement of editors and writers is identified; credit for illustrations is given in the small print of the paragraphs about publication data. While the reader is likely to browse through an issue for the pictures, as with the parent magazine, here the text is presented in a more varied manner, and the eye easily swerves to take in paragraphs that explain photographs or are boxed to call attention to certain information. The writing is basically solid and authoritative, with care exercised to ensure the information's accuracy.

The table of contents announces 10 or so pieces, several of which are monthly regulars. "Kids Did It!" reports unusual activities or accomplishments of individual youngsters who have excelled as storyteller, bowler, golfer, rodeo star, or organist, and groups of youngsters making news by naming a stream or winning at lacrosse. On the back cover, "What in the World?" offers about nine color photographs (sometimes close-ups) to identify. Usually, contests are announced or winners named. Drawings by children are published in the "mailbag"; those submitted in color are reproduced in color.

The four articles of the January 1990 issue are typical of the breadth and treatment of a subject. "Rounds About the Zoo," introduced by a snow leopard on the cover, features the animals and a veterinarian of the San Diego Zoo and provides in illustration and text a clear understanding of the work the woman must do. "Rivers of Ice" on the contents page (but "Glaciers: Huge Rivers of Ice" at the article) predictably shows some stunning shots but also provides a drawing to explain how glaciers are formed and a world map marking "icescapes." "Big Buildups" pictures buildings in the shape of a fish, shoes, a hat, and a bulldozer and notes their purposes; the feature also shows some of the gigantic dinosaurs that have been constructed for various reasons. In "Winter Wonders," the St. Paul Winter Carnival is covered. Two double-page spreads bring out the beauty of the ice sculptures and the spectacular display of fireworks at the finale. Other issues have featured sports events, earthquakes, satellites, and a holiday celebration in Denmark, to hint of the "world" in scope. Puzzles and things to make add to the fun of an issue. Occasionally, "supersize pullout pages" that can be opened and posted appear as a supplement.

A little-disputed strength of the magazine is its brilliantly reproduced full-color photographs. The capturing of the subjects, the angles used, and the clarity of presentation all bespeak the skill of experienced photographers. The magazine's pictures captivate—from the close-ups of the front covers to the magnifications of the back covers that demand scrutiny to solve a puzzle. The aim to bring a *world* of interesting information to children is well met.

National Geographic World is made available on audio disc recording by the Library of Congress.   *Children's Magazine Guide*

Newstime see *Scholastic Newstime*

Odyssey
Kalmbach Publishing Co.
21027 Crossroads Circle, P.O. Box 1612, Waukesha, WI 53187
Monthly; $21

Subtitled "Space Exploration and Astronomy for Young People," this monthly features observational astronomy, astronomical discoveries, and explorations in space, including the technology that makes such ventures possible. Prepared especially for children ages 8 to 14, the major articles offer writing distinguished for clarity and pursuit of accuracy and illustrations that are first-rate in content and expression. The authors write in a style that is solid, instructive, and engaging; they are careful and precise in their descriptions and explanations.

Over half of every issue is apportioned to illustrations: reproductions of photographs and paintings, drawings, diagrams, cartoons, and sky charts. Many of the photographs are from observatories, the National Aeronautics and Space Administration (NASA), and other federal agencies. Some of the 40 pages of this highly pictorial 8⅛-by-10¾-inch monthly are in full color; others are highlighted by a color. Throughout, there is evidence of attention to details of layout and design.

The contents pages list from three to seven major articles called "Features." In a recent issue, the cover story, "It Came from Outer Space," about new products and processes derived from the experiments of space technology, is followed by a one-page quiz, "Spin-off Match-up." Among other features in the issue are "The Stars Down Under," a four-page discussion about viewing the sky from the southern hemisphere, and "How Fast Are You?," a two-page challenge to the reflexes. "Star Search" requires identifying 27 constellations in a black-and-white picture. Coverage is given to some Girl Scouts who worked toward badges with a "Sleepover at the Planetarium." The final feature of this particular issue tells of a musical review about the early days of the U.S. space program and gives the dates and cities of its upcoming tour.

Another recent issue carries three articles about space-education summer camps. One feature introduces such camps pictorially, along with a directory; another offers generous tips from two youngsters who attended space camp; and the third, about vacations that include space or astronomy, prints snapshots and paragraphs from eight subscribers, several of whom attended camp. Other feature articles have explored planets, reported on space missions, and dealt with black holes and brown dwarfs.

Nearly a dozen departments appear regularly, some every month. Among them are three about Ulysses the robot. In the role of assistant to the editor, Ulysses 4-11 authors "Ulysses Speaks" in which thoughts about the magazine (or its subject) or one particular issue are introduced. In "Ulysses I/O Port" (I/O stands for input/output), responses are made to questions and comments from subscribers. "Adventures of Ulysses" is a one-page serialized cartoon. "Dateline: Space" brings news about the latest international developments regarding space, and "What's Up" reports the sky observations of special interest during the month. The beginner is offered help in looking at the constellations in "Star Cards"; "Starry Sky" gives the sky chart for the month. "All-Stars" usually acquaints readers with the Greek myths; the stories about Orion, the Pleiades, and Aquarius have been retold, to name a few.

"Future Forum" consistently presents a topic worth thinking about and reports the responses of readers. Often the topic is quite debatable: Should more resources be devoted to the search for aliens (from outer space)? Sometimes the subject is speculative: What kinds of food will people eat in 200 years? Although the caption has changed over the years, there is usually a place in the magazine for contributions from subscribers in the form of drawings, poems, puzzles, and reports of sky observations. "Planet Plaza" promotes products such as books, calendars, models, and posters.

Odyssey is meant to be a young person's guide to the stars, to the excitement of today's space exploration and discoveries, and to space challenges of the future. The only magazine for young people fully devoted to this subject, fortunately, the magazine excels even without competition. The magazine claims to unlock the universe "with sparkling photos and drawings, with exciting activities and experiments, with superb articles." And that it does! Children already interested in astronomy and outer space will find much to absorb them in the magazine; however, the monthly will undoubtedly be attractive to browsers too who could easily be drawn into the explanations of the pictured phenomena. Because the readership is 85 percent male, parents and librarians should make a special effort to get this magazine into the hands of girls.

Founding editor Nancy Mack has met many deadlines during the past decade but reports that she still enjoys her job. She notes that "the real world of astronomy and space exploration is every bit as exciting as anything Batman or Barbie can cook up." Children (and adults too) can be thankful for her enthusiasm and willingness to bring the marvelous down to earth in a very informative magazine.   *Children's Magazine Guide*

OWL
Young Naturalist Foundation
Edit: 56 The Esplanade, Toronto, ON, M5E 1A7 Canada
Subs: P.O. Box 11314, Des Moines, IA 50340
Monthly; except July and August (10 issues)
$14.95; in Canada, $17

No longer limited to the outdoors and wildlife, from whence it got its name, this "Discovery Magazine for Children" ages 9 to 12 has presented articles on other sciences too and on technology. The 32 pages carry absorbing pieces and suggest projects children can undertake. The layout is varied, uncrowded, and attractive; full color is used most effectively throughout. The 8¼-by-10¾-inch monthly, printed on glossy paper, uses some drawings and cartoons, but by far the most prominent and dramatic of the illustrations are the color photographs. The animal centerfold, a monthly feature, is often a close-up shot that has in the past captured beady eyes or needlelike whiskers. The lure of the cover is a fitting clue to the worthwhile content of this magazine based on "interactive" principles. The emphasis is on nonfiction; only occasionally is there a fiction story.

The Young Naturalist Foundation, publisher of *OWL*, "aims to encourage children to read for enjoyment and discovery; to help children learn more about their country and the world around them; to stimulate children to enjoy, respect and conserve their natural environment; and to give children a wealth of ideas to use constructively." The material between the covers certainly has the potential to lead to the fulfillment of these aims. The magazine maintains high editorial and artistic standards that should enable children to learn about the world around them in an enjoyable way.

This is a magazine of such quality and content that adults too can be readily hooked by the engaging features. Who could resist the centerfold close-up of the snowy owl, tamandua, or galloping zebras? How many adults, drawn into the puzzles and finding the challenge sufficient, will be indebted to the answer page? Or would adults, in reading about a pride of lions and the hunt or a twelve-year-old's trip to the North Pole with his father, become so absorbed that they would forget this is a magazine for children? Truly, *OWL* is the rare publication that brings pleasure and information to the curious of all ages.

A few examples might suggest some of the worlds the magazine encourages youngsters to discover and how the subject matter is conveyed in print and picture. A recent issue features on the cover the winning entry of the annual cover contest drawn by an eight-year-old girl. Six runners-up are shown in miniature on the first pages. The issue is of interest for its special articles, clever puzzles, and stunning photographs. In addition to the centerfold of this issue, the head of a hippo (eyes and snout) pops out of the water, filling the space of a double-page spread. The photograph is followed by a two-page multiple-choice quiz with plenty of humorous possibilities from which to choose. An article about animals that eat ants includes the ones typically thought of but also the echidna, pangolin, and numbat. Brief paragraphs describe the hunting and eating techniques of each animal and its unusual characteristics. A double-page comical drawing asks for the group name of the cavorting animals; hints are given in the picture. (A pod of seals is rowing in a pea pod; a cast of hawks flies with legs encased in plaster.)

In the same issue is a two-part article, "The Deep," about diving. The first part shows some of the early suits worn and mentions the dreaded bends; by turning the magazine, the reader can see in full the latest yellow, molded suit extraordinaire and read about the things the diver can do while wearing it. Flipping the page up, the reader comes upon the second part of the article and a two-page sperm whale diving. Paragraphs around the drawing tell of the whale's incredible diving capabilities and the many ways it can outdistance human divers. The text in all issues is consistently informative and interesting. The style of writing is at once straightforward and entertaining. Clarity and liveliness prevail. Readers are frequently drawn into the content with thought-provoking questions; no infantile pandering exists here. Full color is used on all the pages, whether for photographs or drawings.

Among the regular monthly features readers can look forward to is a four-page cartoon story, "Mighty Mites," the adventures of Nick, Sophie, and Mark Mite who can shrink to any size, a useful trick for exploring a spider web, optical illusions, or the stem of a flower. Another regular is Dr. Zed, a scientist wearing colorful apparel, who in cartoon-like illustrations explains and gives directions for making no-fry fries (to study the gelatinization range of starch molecules), teaches about water resistance, or tests tension and friction. Despite the frivolity suggested by the pictures, the professor behind the article assures that all the experiments are safe for children to do on their own, that no special equipment is required, and that the feature encourages children to be inventive.

"Hoot Club News" at the back of an issue publishes contributions from children, particularly those who have taken an active part in protecting and improving the environment. The magazine sponsors the Hoot Club Awards Program, which recognizes children who undertake projects to save the environment. Among other items on the four pages are brief reports about unusual facts, suggestions of books to read, puzzles, and surveys including the questionnaires and results. A secret message is presented although not decoded in the issue, but the subscriber who requests a Hoot Club Action Pack and Membership (free) will also receive the secret code. The winning color photographs of a contest attest to the skill and creativity of readers. Other contests require writing poetry or stories and drawing pictures. The back cover, captioned "Whatsit?: An Eye-dentification Puzzle," often pictures a half dozen items close-up that need to be named. Answers are usually within the issue; however, one cover was turned into a contest.

The magazine's games, puzzles, and activities are quite varied, and in a year's subscription, many types are offered: board games, crossword puzzles, word and math queries (including geometric ones), tricks with science or logic applications, and the breezy what's-wrong-with-this-picture exercise. Often these challenges rise above the typical because something clever is added to make them innovative or imaginative.

An index is available covering the years from 1976, when *OWL* was first published, to 1987. The magazine is also available in French, entitled *Hibou*, from Les Éditions Héritage Inc., 300 avenue Arran, Saint-Lambert, Quebec, J4K 1K5, Canada. For children under nine, see *Chickadee*. An Italian edition is named *L'Orsa*.   *Children's Magazine Guide*

Pack-o-Fun
Clapper Communications
14 Main St., Park Ridge, IL 60068
Quarterly; $6

Under the nameplate of this 8⅜-by-5⅜-inch magazine is the phrase that encapsulates the content of the quarterly: "Crafts, games and fun for kids!" Most of the 48 pages are filled with clever and simple craft ideas. Puzzles, including a crossword puzzle in each issue, and skits add to the pleasure. Among the regularly appearing items are "Kids in the Kitchen," with unusual but edible snacks (pumpkin popcorn balls and leprechaun punch, for example); "Pen Pals," giving names, addresses, and three interests; and "Next in POF," listing the items to start saving for the next issue's projects. The editor's page would be of more interest to adults than children.

The craft items, however, are the main feature of this magazine. Concise and clear instructions are made specific by black-and-white drawings. Many of the suggestions are seasonal or for certain holidays. At these times, many children are anxious to make decorations and gifts. As many as two dozen items on the contents page lead to projects. Some of the entries give instructions for several things to make. (Counting the number of projects between the covers of an issue is its own game.) The materials for creating the objects are inexpensive and readily available; many of the raw materials would end up in the garbage if not salvaged for these projects.

Readers who want to make an itsy-bitsy spider toy, Cinderella's autumn coach, a Bible-verse basket, an egg carton Christmas tree, a Valentine mailbox, a paper plate Easter lily, or a cornucopia of other novelties, should begin saving spools, plastic detergent bottles, paper bags, foam meat trays, scraps of felt, coffee cans, milk cartons, corks, onion bags, cardboard rolls, feathers, yarn, and the like and then place a subscription for this magazine.

Penny Power
Consumers Union of United States, Inc.
Edit: 256 Washington St., Mount Vernon, NY 10553
Subs: P.O. Box 54861, Boulder, CO 80322
Bimonthly
$11.95; $4.50 each for 10 or more subscriptions to same address

"A Consumer Reports publication" for children, this magazine provides information and advice about using money wisely. Products are tested and rated by the Consumers Union, which uses students in 30 classes around the country for the research team. Some of the half dozen articles of an issue analyze the commodities of which children are readily acknowledged consumers: bubble gum, electronic games, and sneakers, for example. The characteristics and quality of various brands are described and ranked. Other articles might deal with finding jobs, telephone hotlines, and making reports. The accounts are highly pictorial, using photographs, charts, and cartoon-like drawings. The magazine's overall appearance is flashy and cluttered, suitable to the taste of many 8-to-14-year-olds, the intended audience. The 32 semiglossy pages of a colorful 8¼-by-10⅞-inch issue also carry about eight regular departments.

In a recent issue, the product examined is cola, although there is also information about acquiring pocket-sized pets. Points to consider, as well as encouragement, are offered in an article about making things to sell and turning talent into dollars. Selecting a team sport for participation is explored; boxed items delineate risk of injury and cost of equipment, among other matters. The lead article is about "first aid" for party disasters, that is, things to do when a gathering starts to lose its zip. Another article, further along in the issue, suggests ways to say no to drinking at parties.

Several departments appear regularly. "Pen Power," inside the front cover, publishes letters from young consumers about some of their experiences including economical things they have done. A psychiatrist answers other letters in "I've Got a Question," giving advice on everything from making friends to resolving problems with teachers. "P.P.B. Squad" (the bug squad) takes a humorous look at advertising that bugs readers. "The Penny Power Club" is a two-page cartoon story about some friends who help one another handle their consumer or personal problems. Children review television shows and movies. "Commercial Break" spoofs selected advertisements.

Full color is used for the snappy cover. Touches of color or background tints are added to many pages; about half the pages use full color in the pictorial matter, particularly for the photographs. Pages show great variety, and the text is always portioned out in small amounts.

The intent to involve youngsters in consumer decisions pervades the magazine. As a brochure explains, "respect for youngsters' desire for credible and complete information is now a cornerstone of *Penny Power*." Children are not told what to do but are given the encouragement and information necessary to make their own decisions, not only about products but also about such economic matters as budgeting an allowance, distinguishing facts from claims, saving for special purchases, understanding product labels, and even writing letters of complaint.

The editor indicates that some revisions will soon be made in the magazine, but its focus will remain the same. The title is to be changed to *Zillions* in August 1990. (A penny doesn't seem to have much power anymore.) Most likely, regular departments will also be renamed.

Children's Magazine Guide

Piano Explorer
   Accent Publishing Co.
   200 Northfield Rd., Northfield, IL 60093
   Monthly; except June and August (10 issues)
   $6; $3 each for 5 or more subscriptions to same address
Usually ordered and distributed through piano teachers, Clavier's *Piano Explorer* is available by individual subscription and allows a home or library to receive the only music magazine targeted for children. Although

intended to please the young pianist, several of the 14 pages in each issue of this attractive magazine enter realms of music not limited to the piano. An inviting cover, an appealing layout, informative and decorative illustrations, and appropriate touches of color add up to a delightful introduction to music for children in upper elementary grades.

In the three issues examined, two articles that might be of special interest to pianists are "Improving Performance," about gaining confidence, control, and concentration, and "The Page-Turner," about responsibilities and techniques. Three articles of a more general nature include one about western composers who have been inspired by, and incorporated into their pieces, music from the Orient and Africa. Another article is about impressionism in art, particularly the work of Monet, and in music, especially the compositions of Debussy. The third article reveals the unusual circumstances that led to the composing of "Jingle Bells."

Biographical entries a page or two in length give brief accounts about Telemann, Ravel, Bruckner, and Mahler. Bach is given major emphasis in an article about Baroque musicians. Among the instruments given special attention are the trombone, organ, and flute. The article about the flute tells of its history and how it is played; it is accompanied by a full-page, full-color photograph of James Galway in Pied Piper costume. And a reader need not be a piano player to be intrigued by the inner parts of a piano and how a piano is tuned.

Issues usually carry brief music theory lessons. Intervals and scales are discussed, for example. Seemingly, two beginner pieces for the piano are printed in each issue. Most of these compositions (five of six) are submitted by children ages 8 to 12 in issues studied. Among the regular short items are a monthly list of birthdays of musicians, mostly deceased, and a quiz on the content of the issue. Word puzzles and such divertissements as "Name that Tune" round out the 8¼-by-11-inch pages.

Not to be overlooked are the full-color covers and their diversity. One is a watercolor drawing of a cardinal on a wintry branch looking through a window to a baby grand; another, the spectacular pipes of a Baroque organ; the third, two teddy bears playing a four-hand duet on electronic keyboard.

Pilot see *Scholastic News: Pilot*

Playmate see *Children's Playmate Magazine*

Plays
> 120 Boylston St., Boston, MA 02116
> Monthly; October–May, except one issue for January/February (7 issues)
> $23

Each issue of "The Drama Magazine for Young People," *Plays*' subtitle, typically presents three plays designated for junior and senior high and three or more for middle and lower grades. Most issues carry a "dramatized classic." Occasionally, the cover, which also serves as contents page, lists a skit, musical classic, or "curtain raiser." The plays for children can be generally characterized as simple comedies, dramatizations of realistic situations, fanciful stories, light mysteries, and playlets with roots in folklore. Seasonal and holiday productions are included when relevant. For each play, there are stage directions and production notes. Subscribers may produce the plays royalty-free (provided the performance is part of a regular school or dramatic club activity) and may make copies of individual plays for members of the cast. Copyright restrictions are spelled out on the verso of the front cover.

The plays can usually be produced without elaborate staging or overwhelming responsibilities for leading characters. Frequently, the number of cast members can be enlarged by upping the number of extras and walkons. Stage directions are printed in italic; all typefaces are clear and legible. Production notes succinctly specify the number of characters and their sex, playing time (between 15 and 30 minutes), costumes, properties, setting, lighting, and sound. No illustrations are provided, which is as it should be, because the acting companies will learn more by creating their own costumes and sets than by replicating something shown.

The four plays for middle and lower grades in a recent issue all have their underlying humor, as well as some outlandish lines that talented young actors might well deliver in a way that would cause audiences to roll over in laughter. (Serious drama is probably best left to seasoned actors anyway.) Scripts must be brought to life, and directors will certainly play influential roles in this regard with "Sgt. Dobetter's Deep Freeze," set in the barren wasteland of the frozen north with no fewer than four Mounties in the cast. An inclination for actors to deliver lines for the laugh will have to be tempered by an intent to move the plot along. A few lines might be improved by rewriting. Some remarks seem adult-like but probably wouldn't be entirely lost on children. In another play, a librarian solves the mystery of "Who Killed Doc Robbins," the dentist. Aileen Fisher wrote one of the holiday plays of the issue, "Hearts, Tarts and Valentines." Set in the Kingdom of the King and Queen of Hearts, the play makes considerable use of a narrator, a technique the skilled author uses to advantage. In "A February Failure," sluggish Harry Hardwick eventually prepares his assignment, a poem about a man who overcame failures, Abe Lincoln. In the same issue, the dramatized classic is "Dracula," and a curtain raiser is titled "Astro Annie," a space-age melodrama.

The May issue carries an author-title index to the plays of the volume, sorted under "for junior and senior high" and "for middle and lower grades." A subject index in one alphabet groups plays by topic and type. Major holidays and celebrations are listed by their specific names. Other typical subjects are health and nutrition, biography, and computers. About two dozen plays are named under comedies and farces and another two dozen under dramas. Nearly 10 plays are identified as mysteries and suspense and another 10 as skits, spoofs, and curtain raisers. About five plays fall into each of the following classifications: melodrama; patriotic and historical; classic; fantasy; and folktale, fairy tale, and legend. A look at the categories of the subject index suggests the types of plays available in an annual subscription.

About 80 plays are printed during a year in the 64 pages (80 in two issues) of this 5½-by-8½-inch magazine. Because only a few of the productions in an issue are closely tied to a particular month, a subscription offers variety and choices and should fulfill requests from aspiring thespians. While too many lines are more equal than superior to those of television sitcoms, in certain plays there is an element of suspense in moving to the denouement. Some dialogue is stilted and verses are strained, but if clever youngsters are given license to improvise, they will undoubtedly improve upon the script. *Children's Magazine Guide*

Prehistoric Times
Troll Associates
100 Corporate Dr., Mahwah, NJ 07430
8 issues a year
$9.95

A slim magazine that capitalizes on the sustained interest in dinosaurs and satisfies the thirst for the spectacular flashes on its covers such lines as "Big Brushing Job," "Terror of the Prehistoric World," and "The Big Fight." Color is used throughout the eight pages. Readers ages four to eight, are addressed by the editors just inside the wraparound mailer. All material is gathered by the editorial staff; however, consultants sometimes are acknowledged.

Most of the informational pieces and puzzles are a page or two in length and are generously illustrated with drawings. Among regularly appearing items are a profile of a paleontologist and instructions for drawing a dinosaur. One page is captioned "Puzzles-n-Riddles." Each issue contains a dot-to-dot picture.

The 8⅜-by-10⅞-inch pages are filled to capacity, many with the antics of dinosaurs. Young children fascinated by long names and interested in dinosaur facts will derive pleasure from this magazine published since 1987. Occasionally, coverage is given to matters not specifically dinosaurian, such as redwood trees and the giant ground sloth.

Prima Ballerina
Prima Publishing Group, Inc.
Edit: 5696 Peachtree Pkwy., Norcross, GA 30092
Subs: P.O. Box 77265, Atlanta, GA 33057
Bimonthly; $9.95

A recent entry into a specialized and previously unserved market is this bimonthly that calls itself "The Premier Ballet, Jazz and Tap Magazine for Young Dancers." Many of the 32 glossy-coated pages and the cover carry photographs in full color, including the issue's pages (one out of every three) devoted to ads. Most of the other 8½-by-11-inch pages have decorative touches of color. On the contents page the material of an issue is placed under "Features" or "Departments."

In an early issue, five titles are listed under "Features." All are highly pictorial and a page or two in length. The first three are about the "Nutcracker" as performed by the New York City Ballet. One is about the 10-year-old who recently danced the role of Marie; another tells of Balanchine's production for NYCB; and in the third, a dancer reminisces about the 1954 Balanchine debut. Another feature tells of the Christmas show at Radio City Music Hall starring the Rockettes, and the fifth challenges readers to match a half dozen pairs of dancing shoes with the appropriate dancers. Among the departments in this particular issue are "News from You," drawings and one poem from young dancers; "To the Pointe," an expert's answer to a question posed by a 10-year-old boy; and "Behind the Scenes," describing the need for a ballet dancer to wear her hair up. "The Great Ones" profiles Fred Astaire and "Dancing Feats" highlights the accomplishments of a 13-year-old. "Center Stage" briefly tells of the auditions for children for NYCB's *Nutcracker* and leads to the centerfold, a scene from the production.

The premier issue also places greater emphasis on ballet than on the other dance forms in its subtitle. The nonballet features are about the National Museum of Dance at Saratoga and the star of the movie *Annie*, who is now a freshman in college.

¿Qué tal?
Scholastic Inc.
Edit: 730 Broadway, New York, NY 10003
Subs: 2931 E. McCarty St., P.O. Box 3710, Jefferson City, MO
   65102
6 issues during school year: September/October, November,
   December/January, February, March, and April/May
$9.50; $4.95 each for 10 or more subscriptions to same address

Intended for those learning Spanish, this classroom periodical might also be adapted to some uses in bilingual programs. The beginning magazine is followed by *El Sol* (intermediate) and *Hoy Día* (advanced). Home subscriptions might well be considered when the magazines are not available through libraries or school classrooms. The edition for teachers includes a copy of the student's magazine, teaching suggestions, and answers to puzzles and quizzes. The four-page pamphlet is available free to teachers of classes ordering 10 or more copies of the student edition; a single subscription is $20.

The magazine provides word games, puzzles, and picture stories with content of interest to early adolescents. In one issue, the cover photograph shows a scene from an Indiana Jones film being shot in Spain. (A short paragraph and black-and-white photograph say more about the film inside; the teacher's edition poses five questions about the cover.) A World Cup soccer game is the subject of the first feature, which brings three exciting full-color photographs. Another story highlights the teenagers of a Cuban boarding school, a place in the country where the young adults help harvest the citrus crop. The centerfold of this issue features a large deserted island surrounded by word puzzles.

Biographical material about sports and media figures with Hispanic backgrounds is regularly carried. "Garfield" is currently running "en español." Photo stories provide further opportunities to use the language. Games and other vocabulary-building activities are likely to be found on any of the 12 pages. Thus, entertaining reading, skill-building activities, and cultural enrichment are packed between the full-color covers while allowing easily two-thirds of the space for color illustrations—photographs, cartoons, and drawings.

Das Rad
Scholastic Inc.
Edit: 730 Broadway, New York, NY 10003
Subs: 2931 E. McCarty St., P.O. Box 3710, Jefferson City, MO 65102
6 issues during school year: September/October, November, December/January, February, March, and April/May
$9.50; $4.95 each for 10 or more subscriptions to same address

For classes studying German, this is the beginning-level periodical. (For intermediate students, there is *Schuss*.) The 12 pages offer pictures, games, articles, and views of German-speaking countries and their peoples. Puzzles and other word games are intended to strengthen facility with German. The format is similar to other Scholastic periodicals, especially those in French and Spanish. Published on newsprint, pages are either full color or have touches of color added. Photographs, particularly those of peers, are a pleasing feature of the monthly.

Attuned to interests of older children and those in junior high, cover stories feature entertainment personalities and figures of the sports world. "Wie geht's?" brings letters and snapshots from subscribers. In issues examined, the cartoon story of the last page is from the adventures of Detective A. Meise (Anna, that is). A German-English vocabulary in each issue provides aid with the content. Of course, the many illustrations also give clues.

The answers to puzzles are not always included in the student edition, which would suggest one reason a teacher (or parent) might want to subscribe to the edition for teachers. This edition costs $20 but is free with 10 or more student subscriptions. A copy of the student's magazine is included in the edition for teachers.

Rainbow
Ukrainian National Association, Inc.
30 Montgomery St., Jersey City, NJ 07302
Monthly; except bimonthly May–August (10 issues)
$8

Published in Ukrainian, this monthly might have a limited number of subscribers, but it is heartening to learn of such a magazine. The 16 pages are filled with stories, articles, verses, and pictorial matter. Among the fiction stories are tales of animals, and among the nonfiction articles are biographical pieces. Both the humorous and the historical are spotlighted, as well as seasonal events and celebrations. Several touches of color are used in an issue; even text is sometimes printed in color. Drawings and photographs are the primary illustrations of the 8½-by-11-inch pages. One issue brings a song—music accompaniment included—on the back cover. Intended for ages 3 to 12, the length of some articles suggests material targeted for the upper end of the range, while short verses and comical drawings will probably please the young. All readers must understand Ukrainian to enjoy *Veselka*, published since 1954.

Ranger see *Scholastic News: Ranger*

Ranger Rick
National Wildlife Federation
8925 Leesburg Pike, Vienna, VA 22184
Monthly; $14

For ages 6 to 12 and targeted at nine-year-olds, this splendid highly pictorial monthly teaches children about wildlife, natural history, natural science, and the environment. The magazine is "dedicated to inspiring a greater understanding and appreciation of the natural world in a creative and entertaining way." Readers in awe of the stunning full-color photographs of the covers, front and back, will find astonishing the many close-ups of fish and fowl, insects and mammals, on the glossy paper inside. The articles are informative and lucidly written. Nature projects are suggested and explained in sufficient detail that children might accomplish them. Ranger Rick is a raccoon. The monthly is sold on a membership basis. Preschoolers are expected to move from *Your Big Backyard* to this magazine.

The half dozen articles of a recent issue suggest the coverage typical of the monthly. The lead story is a first-person account of the difficulties a photographer has shooting koalas in Australia. The text reveals information about the habits and habitat of the koala; three photographs attest to why people think the animal cuddly. A feature on the porcupine fish begins with a double-page spread of one fully puffed in close-up. The following page tells about this unusual characteristic of puffers and its usefulness. The article closes with pages about the Japanese yen for eating fugu. The next three pages provide instructions for making a clever porcupine fish from a paper cutout into which is inserted a balloon. An eight-page article about threatened birds of prey includes a striking centerfold of the head of a sharp-eyed golden eagle. Smaller head shots picture hawks and falcons. Efforts to protect these birds are briefly reported in the text. In another article, the devastation of the Alaskan oil spill is captured in the close-up photograph of a small oil-drenched bird. Ten children provide one-paragraph commentaries (one is a poem) on the effect of the accident on the environment; six of the children live in the area. The last pages picture "Wild Ways to Catch a Meal," showing a sawbill snap a fish and a marsh mongoose grab a crab. Two series of color photographs reveal the action in an encounter of a sea star with an anemone and a kingfisher after its prey. All of these articles are fully illustrated with full-color marvelous photographs. One article uses humorous drawings to accompany a text about how animals keep warm in winter (the article calls it "chubby warmth," or blubber). A final page describes the warming "tricks" of a polar bear (the illustration shows the bear in beach attire).

Features that appear regularly in the magazine's 48 pages are "Adventures of Ranger Rick," stories about the raccoon and his woodland friends who set off to solve various environmental problems, and letters to the magazine. In "Dear Ranger Rick," readers write about experiences they've had similar to ones reported in previous issues. "Who-o-o Knows?" publishes questions from readers for which Wise Old Owl knows the answers. Usually, there is a page or two of puzzles. A page-and-a-half full-color photograph always shares beginning pages with the listing of contents. The contents page title for an article does not always have the same wording as the title found at the article. The front and back covers for years have featured superb full-color portraits of members of the animal kingdom. Tree frog, mandarin duck, yak, katydid, spiny mouse, or bear— all invite close inspection; few could be viewed so closely (or for any length of time) in their habitats.

Some of the members of the animal kingdom spotted within the covers of a single issue are a sea lion, blue fin tuna, white weasel, raccoon and cubs, cougar, red crab, sea otter, spur-winged plover, web-footed gecko, beetle, spider, gerbil, and an adder. Consider the natural habitats of these creatures to grasp the world-wide explorations of this magazine and to note that land, sea, and air are within the purview of the magazine's mission. The articles are authored by staff and others. The writing is factual, readable, and convincing. Occasionally, an issue will carry a feature on people—for example, the inhabitants of a South Pacific island. People— children and adults—are shown in some illustrations, and their endeavors to save and improve the environment provide copy for the text.

Would that all children were familiar with this fine magazine and its younger sibling, *Your Big Backyard*. A first-rate introduction to nature, *Ranger Rick* also acquaints children with the best of color photography and helps them develop reading skills via fascinating subject matter. Meticulous attention to concept and detail surely underlies every page. What else of such value can be purchased for a child at about $1.20 a month?

Ranger Rick is available on audio disc recording through the National Library Service for the Blind and Physically Handicapped, Library of Congress.   *Children's Magazine Guide*

Read
Field Publications
Edit: 245 Long Hill Rd., Middletown, CT 06457
Subs: 4343 Equity Dr., Columbus, OH 43228
Biweekly during school year (18 issues)
$12.50; $6.25 each for 10 or more subscriptions to same address
Above the nameplate of this digest-sized biweekly, its language-arts emphasis is made clear in the line, "The Magazine for Reading and

English." Intended for grades 6 to 10 (reading levels 5.5–7), the editors seek to provide content with appeal to junior high students. Issues bring with seeming regularity a play and a short story, and "Wrap-Up," which checks up on the reader's comprehension of both. The play is often a simplified version of an upcoming television drama; the PBS "Wonderworks" series is represented in issues examined. Throughout the year, other forms of writing—narrative and essay, for example—are included in various issues. The expository writing usually deals with a contemporary concern such as experiments on animals or the world's future. Over a period of time, readers have opportunities to sample the works of such respected writers as Edgar Allan Poe, H. G. Wells, and Isaac Asimov, to name three.

The initial pages in each issue bring "In Your Own Write," the poetry contributions of students. Several pages at the back hold puzzles and games that help students learn or review grammar, spelling, vocabulary, punctuation, and other language-arts skills. One issue annually is devoted entirely to work of students, usually short stories. The contest that draws in the contributions also accepts plays, poetry, artwork, photography, and puzzles.

A member of the Field family, this 32-page classroom periodical is the only Field publication that is 5¼ by 8¼ inches in size. The magazine is printed on newsprint and uses drawings and sometimes black-and-white photographs to illustrate features. The cover is always pictorial. A color, or two of its shades, is used throughout an issue to highlight captions and titles, to frame or box content, and to provide a color background for certain pages. The magazine has a few visual enticements. Typeface is clear and legible.

A guide for the teacher supplies discussion questions and pages that exercise reading, listening, and writing skills, pages that can be reproduced to distribute to students. An index for the school year is printed in the final issue of the teacher's guide.

The Real Ghostbusters Magazine
Welsh Publishing Group, Inc.
Edit: 300 Madison Ave., New York, NY 10017
Subs: P.O. Box 10176, Des Moines, IA 50340
Quarterly; $7.80

This magazine, published since 1989, will be around as long as Ghostbusters are the rage. A fun-filled quarterly that replicates as best it can the special effects and gadgets of the *Ghostbusters* movies, this one, as some others in the Welsh line, announces "Features" and "In Every Issue" on the contents page. The cover is an action-packed drawing of the four Ghostbusters: zany Peter, serious Egon, lovable Ray, and dependable Winston. More of their daring do is portrayed in the flashy colors of the centerfold poster. The faithful secretary Janine and the pet ghost Slimer also put in appearances. Ads are as lively as the other content and take up a half dozen pages at front and back of an issue. Intended for ages 6 to 11, the 32 colorful pages will be most warmly received by the foursome's fans.

Among the regular items are "Ghostly Greetings," the introduction to the issue by a member of the quartet, and "Who You Gonna Write?", letters of praise from readers to the magazine and its characters. "Egon's Science and Tech Report" briefly describes scientific matters such as magnetically levitated trains, robots, the shape of igloos, and the weaving of spider webs. "Boredom Busters" notifies readers of new movies and books, contests, and special events. The last page of an issue carries jokes in "Dr. Venkman's Gag File."

Every issue brings a four-page comic strip of the Real Ghostbusters in action and a three-page adventure from their casebook. In a more informative vein, pictorial articles have described fire stations, unusual places of the world, and prospects for the future. The rest of the pieces, as well as those mentioned in the previous paragraph, are a page or two in length. Among the puzzles are those using words, including crossword puzzles. Instructions for drawing and coloring pictures are given on some pages, while on others, hidden pictures are to be found. A rebus story and board game are presented in one issue examined.

Reflections
Journalism Class, Duncan Falls Junior High
P.O. Box 368, Duncan Falls, OH 43734
Semiannual: May and January
$5

Published twice a year by seventh- and eighth-grade students and edited by their English teacher, this magazine accepts primarily poetry. About 35 poems appear in an issue. Most of the offerings are from children ages 12 to 14; about one-third come from Ohio, the rest from all parts of the country. A black-and-white photograph of the contributor often accompanies the submission, along with age, school and location, and, usually, name of teacher. In issues examined, poems by girls outnumber those by boys about three to one. At least one short story is printed in an issue; some issues print more. Essays, plays, and humorous articles are also accepted. Some issues carry an interview with an adult poet or writer. Other issues outline ideas for teaching a writing program.

The content is indicative of the diversity of feelings, experiences, and understandings among the young. The writing varies from the derivative and ordinary to the perceptive and unusual. Some rhymes falter; other word combinations are delicious. Humor and seriousness find expression. On a single page in one particular issue, a nine-year-old speaks of war and peace and another youngster of unicorns in a crystal forest. Much use is made of first person, a fitting way to encourage original work. Even so, among the egocentric lines are such charming clauses as, "when I was a Knight in Sir Lancelot's army."

Ample space is given on the 8½-by-11-inch pages for the poems and photographs of contributors. Decoration is appropriately held to a minimum. Two typefaces are used, even on adjacent pages; one lacks clarity. The arrangement of the content of the 32 pages (sometimes 36) is seemingly dictated by the contributors' ages, beginning with the youngest.

The magazine was started in 1981 by Dean Harper, who continues as editor. Duncan Falls Junior High enrolls 300 students in grades seven and eight. It identifies itself as "one of the little red brick schoolhouses where time has had little influence" in a school district that "ranks at the bottom of the state in money spent per student." Intended for students of all ages, the works of children from ages 6 to 18 have been published in the magazine. While such a publication should not be used in lieu of books introducing children to the finest poets writing for children today, some children are likely to enjoy, and even be inspired by, the verses of contemporaries.

Scholastic Action
Scholastic Inc.
Edit: 730 Broadway, New York, NY 10003
Subs: 2931 E. McCarty St., P.O. Box 3710, Jefferson City, MO
   65102
Biweekly during school year: September–April (14 issues)
$11.50; $5.75 each for 10 or more subscriptions to same address
The publisher targets this magazine at students in grades seven to nine, whose reading levels are at the second to fourth grade. Reflecting the interests and abilities of the readers, the 16-page biweekly brings teen-oriented features, including read-aloud plays, articles, stories, and news, as well as information on careers and activities that build reading skills.

The first pages carry "News Shorts," brief items of current interest. A regular feature is "Close-Up," which has discussed, among other matters, both the census and alcohol abuse. Another is "Lakeville U.S.A.," a five-box cartoon-like story (but color photographs are used) about daily living concerns such as stress management and interviewing skills. The adjacent page offers advice and exercises with regard to the topic. Each issue prints a play for oral reading; oftentimes it is adapted from a book or television presentation. The double issue of one year is devoted to five plays. The back page, captioned "Puzzler," in issues examined, reviews vocabulary of the issue with a two-step puzzle involving definitions and a mystery photo.

The same size, 8 by 10⅞ inches, as other Scholastic periodicals, this one uses color on all pages. Heavy use is made of photographs; teenagers are frequently the subjects. The printed word is particularly legible, no threat to hard-to-please readers, and text is broken down into manageable pieces by boldface insertions. The writing, even within the constraint imposed by reading level, is acceptable and gives sufficient reason to extend the magazine to upper elementary students who are interested in teenage life.

Scholastic Choices
Scholastic Inc.
Edit: 730 Broadway, New York, NY 10003
Subs: 2931 E. McCarty St., P.O. Box 3710, Jefferson City, MO
   65102
Monthly during school year: September–May (9 issues)
$8.75; $5.50 each for 10 or more subscriptions to same address
Although the magazine continues to be categorized under "home economics," there is little resemblance to the former *Co-ed*. The subtitle now

reads, "The Magazine for Personal Development & Practical Living Skills." Among the facets considered in this monthly for grades 7 to 12 are family relationships, health, food and nutrition, and clothing, as well as consumer skills and careers. The contents page regularly places the material of the 36 pages of each 8-by-10½-inch issue under "About You & Others," "Home & Life Skills," and "Departments." Many of the pages (and the ads) are in full color. Touches of color are added to other pages. The color photographs of teenagers in some of the feature articles and the final products of recipes are especially clearly presented.

Among the topics featured in various issues under "About You & Others" are parenting skills, crack cocaine, gaining confidence, preventing violence, and managing stress. The articles under "Home & Life Skills" tend to be about food and nutrition (including recipes), health and safety, and consumer concerns. A recent series finding place sometimes under one heading and sometimes under the other is an "independent-living series" that has followed six high school seniors, addressing such matters as renting their first apartment and making marriages and relationships work. Profiles too have been entered under both categories and tend to spotlight entertainers and sports figures. Regular "Departments" include news items; a crossword puzzle with a theme (herbs and spices, cooking terms, fabric basics); "Fun Food Facts," about bananas, hotdogs, or squash, for example; "Help!", advice from a psychologist; and "Sticky Situation," with one situation presented and a half dozen responses to an earlier one.

The magazine is not intended for children below seventh grade. Some of the content will be of greater importance to senior high students. For junior high students and children in upper elementary grades expressing interest in the magazine's subjects, this classroom periodical suggests some of the choices facing adolescents.   *Children's Magazine Guide*

Scholastic DynaMath
Scholastic Inc.
Edit: 730 Broadway, New York, NY 10003
Subs: 2931 E. McCarty St., P.O. Box 3710, Jefferson City, MO
    65102
Monthly during school year: September–May (9 issues)
$11.70; $5.95 each for 10 or more subscriptions to same address

Targeted for grades five and six, this math monthly offers puzzles and activities to increase facility with such skills as computation and measurement and to build upon the power to reason. All is packaged in a humorous and lively format. There is plenty of math for the money in every 16-page issue. While those children who relish math are likely to gobble up this magazine, surely even those reluctant about matters mathematical will find the amusing circumstances and clear directions quite palatable.

The cover is consistently zestful and inviting. Drawings and photographs bear such come-ons as "Math or Magic?" and "Think or Swim." The first two pages regularly carry "Math Mad," with a miscellany of warm-up puzzles, news items, and number trivia. Two symbols on these pages, and elsewhere in an issue, mark those items that are "tough stuff" and those that have a "calculator option." The framed "Back Page" closes the issue with yet another intriguing puzzle—for example, a crossnumber puzzle.

Several captions appear rather regularly in the issues although in various locations. In "Word Problems," subscribers must work out some of the curious problems facing the ebullient Whimdotters of Digitown. "Practical Math" necessitates calculations involving money and the use of a ruler. In the "Geometry Feature," tessellations and topology, among other topics, are considered. To answer some questions posed in "Fact Finders," young mathematicians need to be able to read tables and timelines. Other pages are captioned "Activity," and therein is presented a great variety of clever and challenging puzzles.

Scholastic, Inc.

Elementary school magazines
Scholastic Let's Find Out   kindergarten
Scholastic News: Pilot   grade 1
Scholastic News: Ranger   grade 2
Scholastic News: Trails   grade 3
Scholastic News: Explorer   grade 4
Scholastic News: Citizen   grade 5
Scholastic Newstime   grade 6
Scholastic Sprint   grades 4–6; reading level grades 2–3
Scholastic DynaMath   grades 5–6
SuperScience Red   grades 1–3
SuperScience Blue   grades 4–6

Secondary school magazines
(excluding those intended for grades 8–12)
Junior Scholastic   grades 6–8
U.S. Express   grades 6–12
Scholastic Action   grades 7–9; reading level grades 2–4
Scholastic Math Magazine   grades 7–9
Science World   grades 7–10
Art & Man   grades 7–12
Scholastic Choices   grades 7–12

Foreign-language magazines
(beginning level only)
French
   Bonjour
German
   Das Rad
Spanish
   ¿Qué Tal?

The company publishes a long line of classroom periodicals, primarily intended for group purchase but available through individual subscription. With ample attention to developing and practicing skills, including those of the problem-solving and basic competency species, the magazines attempt to update and enrich the classroom fare through visually appealing formats and content that is topical. The intent is "to supplement the classroom curricula and to help students understand the issues that shape their lives." Reading and learning activities that build various skills are found in all issues. The publisher claims to reach nine out of ten schools in the United States.

Meant to be weekly newspapers for children, each elementary school magazine is prepared for certain grade levels. Going up the ladder from *Let's Find Out* to *Newstime*, the reading difficulty increases and the worldview broadens. The emphasis on current events is appropriately carried out in the use of many photographs and informative pieces, varying in length for the levels. *Sprint* is designed for children not doing well in school subjects. *Action* is prepared for junior high students having difficulty with reading and is written at elementary school reading levels, although the subject matter is geared to older youngsters. The title might be of interest to children who want to read about teen topics. Two magazines published for elementary grades are subject specific. *DynaMath* seeks to develop math and reasoning skills. *SuperScience*, the most recent title added to the publisher's line, features science but attempts to integrate other curricular areas.

Secondary school magazines intended for children of junior high age focus on curriculum areas. The subjects are sometimes evident in the title: *Art & Man*, *Junior Scholastic* (social studies), *Scholastic Math*, and *Science World*. *Choices* deals with topics quite often addressed in home economics. A few of these magazines are meant for students through the 12th grade; however, any of them could be suggested to children in upper elementary grades who are good readers or are particularly interested in the subjects. Five magazines for secondary school students, not discussed in this book, are *Literary Cavalcade*, *Scholastic Scope*, *Scholastic Search*, *Scholastic Update*, and *Scholastic Voice*.

Foreign-language publications are prepared in three languages for various levels. Although somewhat slanted to secondary students, the monthlies might be of interest to elementary schools that offer French, German, or Spanish and to homes where these languages are encouraged or spoken. Levels roughly approximate years of study, but children might appreciate having some say in choosing the level, particularly with regard to whether they want to be challenged by the vocabulary or to relax with the language. French and Spanish are offered (in addition to the beginning level discussed in this book) at intermediate and advanced levels: in French, *Ça Va* and *Chez Nous*; and in Spanish, *El Sol* and *Hoy Día*. An advanced level of German is not published, but the intermediate-level periodical is titled *Schuss*.

Editions for teachers are printed for all the classroom periodicals, costing about $20, but are sent free to teachers gathering 10 or more subscriptions from students. Teachers submitting bulk orders are also favored with supplementary materials. Within the descriptions in this book of the specific Scholastic titles, mention is occasionally made of the content and utility of the guides for teachers; however, the publisher should be queried for any further information that is needed. Scholastic also publishes several professional magazines for teachers.

Peanut Butter (ages 4–7), *Hot Dog* (ages 6–9), and *Dynamite* (ages 8–12), which used to be sold by single subscription and on newsstands, are now available only on a single-copy basis. The titles must be ordered through Scholastic Book Clubs, found only in schools.

Scholastic Let's Find Out
Scholastic Inc.
Edit: 730 Broadway, New York, NY 10003
Subs: 2931 E. McCarty St., P.O. Box 3710, Jefferson City, MO
65102
Monthly during school year (see below)
$8.50; $4.25 each for 10 or more subscriptions to same address
The introduction to the Scholastic habit, this colorful newspaper is intended for kindergartners (and prekindergartners) and the teachers or parents who will help them become familiar with the practices of classroom periodicals. The 8-by-10⅞-inch monthly, published on newsprint, is divided into four four-page parts, which in a classroom could be apportioned out weekly.

In a year's subscription, the young child is certain to be introduced to seasons and holidays. Other topics generally covered are animals (from tiny ones to dinosaurs) and growth (the kindergartner's own and that of plants and animals). Food and nutrition, transportation, and sky and space are other subjects treated, as well as the affective ones of sharing, working together, and describing feelings. One month brought features on Martin Luther King, Chinese New Year, and Mother Goose.

In the guide for teachers, suggestions for teachers and the student issue's content are categorized by curriculum areas: language arts, social studies, science, math, art, and music and dance. Among the skills addressed are counting, measuring, comparing, classifying, sequencing, rhyming, and matching. Some features allow for learning about storytelling, and others features, according to the editor, promote the scientific method. The fourth page of the student issue is usually captioned "Skills Page" and brings an activity for the young child and a paragraph of suggestions in English and Spanish for parents. Color is used generously throughout. Many colors appear on a page, and even solid colors are sometimes used for backgrounds, masking the off-white of the newsprint. The artwork shows much improvement over earlier issues; line and shape are kept simple, making for strength and clarity. The work of skilled illustrators in some issues, however, is superior to the busy and heavy drawings of other issues. Color photographs are used occasionally. Allowing for white space (or a single color tint) keeps many pages from becoming unsettling to the eye.

The edition for teachers is available at $20 for the school year. This edition includes a copy of the child's edition, posters, a newsletter for parents (in English and Spanish), and "games and task cards."

Scholastic Math Magazine
Scholastic Inc.
Edit: 730 Broadway, New York, NY 10003
Subs: 2931 E. McCarty St., P.O. Box 3710, Jefferson City, MO 65102
Biweekly during school year (14 issues)
$11.70; $5.95 each for 10 or more subscriptions to same address

For students in grades seven to nine, *Math* follows upon *DynaMath* intended for grades five and six. Sixteen pages of every conceivable type of problem and mathematical operation, the biweekly features a superabundance of games, activities, and exercises by which to flex the math muscles. The lively full-color cover primes the mathematician for the content.

Usually, on the verso of the cover is "Hot Stuff," about stars of the entertainment world, which is adjacent to "Short Stuff," a one-page regular of brief items—for example, tricky triangles and MMMs (major math mistakes found in printed works). The two- and three-page features follow. Among those appearing fairly regularly are "Personal Math," for example, using a scale drawing or comparing products; "Test-taking Practice," brushing up on fractions and other facets of math; "Career Feature," one that requires math; and "Problem Solver," logic and word problems. Special stories in issues examined include using a formula and increasing and reducing a recipe. Any one of the articles might require using tables, charts, and graphs; organizing, tallying, and interpreting data; measuring time and space; or estimating and computing.

The same size as most Scholastic periodicals, all pages have touches of color. Photographs are used when appropriate, and elsewhere colorful drawings invite participation. Underlying the color and fun are practice sessions for improving reading, math, and reasoning skills.

The edition for teachers has the answers, and except to those few readers who always score 100 percent, they are essential. If the magazine is purchased for home or library, the subscription price of $20.50 will be a necessary investment. (The edition is free to teachers who order 10 or more subscriptions.) The paragraphs addressed to teachers emphasize the importance of problem solving, stressing that students often know the basic computational skills but stumble when they come to applications and solving problems.

Scholastic News
Five news and current events magazines share this title; distinctions are made by means of subtitle. One more is named *Scholastic Newstime*. A common title, according to the publisher, suggests continuity, a unified program of reading and skills development continuing through six grades. *Pilot*, which is published for the first grade, encourages reading readiness and aids in language development. The subtitles for the successive grades are *Ranger* (grade two), *Trails* (three), *Explorer* (four), and *Citizen* (five). *Newstime* is intended for grade six. Each magazine builds on areas of vocabulary, sentence structure, paragraphing, and critical thinking, depending on the skills applicable

to each particular grade level. In addition, there are supplements centering on themes related to current topics. The entire series is heavily illustrated, much in color, and produced on newsprint. *Citizen* and *Newstime* have become tabloid in size. The publisher takes special efforts to make the magazines appeal to children in content and format. Major national and international developments are covered from the point of view of children who are involved and in ways that show how news events affect the lives of children. "Our goal is to bring the real world into the classroom—in a way that has real meaning for children," maintains the publisher.

Scholastic News: Citizen
Scholastic Inc.
Edit: 730 Broadway, New York, NY 10003
Subs: 2931 E. McCarty St., P.O. Box 3710, Jefferson City, MO
65102
Weekly during school year (26 issues)
$5.00; $2.50 each for 10 or more subscriptions to same address

With this edition for fifth graders, the format of *News* changes to tabloid size, 11⅜ by 16⅜ inches. The newspaper conventions already introduced in editions for primary grades—columns, headlines, signed articles, and photographs—are continued. The four pages are usually printed in full color, although the center pages sometimes use a single color. National and world news that is of interest to children is reported, as well as news that they might well be concerned about. The reports are never lengthy, and pictorial matter is usually equal to text. Much use is made of photographs.

Front-page coverage in recent issues examined each treats three subjects. The headlines of the lead stories suggest that subjects covered in other editions of *News* are also reported here: "South America's War on Drugs," "Unions Striking Out," and "Space Telescope Gives Scientists New Outlook on Universe." The other front page stories tend to be of the human-interest variety. In one issue, illustration and text of the front page feature a fifth grader who invented a biodegradable golf tee that packages grass seed and fertilizer, and Gary Kasparov in his winning chess bout with a computer. On occasion, the center pages of an issue present a double-page spread considered a supplement. One on science about social animals presents three articles (one a comparison of chimps and dolphins, one about a red fire ant colony, and one on the sabertooth cat), some experiments to try, and "Amazing Animal Fun Facts."

Other topics touched upon in recent issues suggest the breadth of coverage of the periodical. On one page, there is a report on the efforts to release caribou into the wild in Maine, and on the next page, the attempts to cut down on wild attire with school dress codes. A full page about famous women depicts Sally Ride, Rosa Parks, Eugenie Clark (marine biologist), Susette LaFlesche (who spoke for the rights of native Americans in the 1800s), Linda Bray (captain in command in a Panama battle), and Victoria Brucker (first female player in the Little League World Series).

The bottom half of the back page brings the exercises. "News and Vocabulary Review" and "Words of the Week" (definitions) seemingly have specific locations. A crossword puzzle, logic puzzle, or word test usually fills out the section.

Whether purchased for the classroom, library, or home, this colorful periodical could help children learn to appreciate the benefits of reading newspapers—except that *News* is lacking, mercifully, the ads, obits, and gossip.

Scholastic News: Explorer
Scholastic Inc.
   Edit: 730 Broadway, New York, NY 10003
   Subs: 2931 E. McCarty St., P.O. Box 3710, Jefferson City, MO
      65102
   Weekly during school year (26 issues)
   $4.50; $2.25 each for 10 or more subscriptions to same address
Explorer, before *Citizen* and after *Trails*, is prepared primarily for fourth graders. The weekly issues are now expanded from four to eight pages, but the 8-by-10⅞-inch newsprint publication builds on newspaper practices introduced in earlier editions. The amount of text increases as the size of print decreases. The illustrations are mostly color photographs.

The front page is about two-thirds picture and one-third text; it also carries a brief index to the content. The story introduced here is continued on page two under the caption, "Front-page News." Among recent cover-story headlines are "Colombia Fights Back against Drugs," "On Strike," and "Space Telescope Is Exciting New Tool." Authorship is given to the articles. The accounts are quite readable, both interesting and informative. Center pages provide the reader with supplements about such subjects as social animals—dolphins, chimps, and ants, for example; zoo news; how money is made; or with a study-skills test. Other topics scattered in issues examined include snowshoe softball and the problems of illiteracy.

"Words of the Week" brings together the words in articles that some readers might need defined. Exercises over a period of time are likely to require reading charts, graphs, and maps; choosing among several items; filling in blanks; and making calculations. The last page frequently tests readers on the content with "News and Vocabulary Review." A continuing challenge, at two a week, is "Guess the States." A calendar for the month carries typical data about specific dates and national weeks and a few riddles, questions, and trivia, for which the answers are provided, upside down, at the bottom of the page.

The edition for teachers continues the content and format of the guides described for magazines for younger children.

Scholastic News: Pilot
Scholastic Inc.
Edit: 730 Broadway, New York, NY 10003
Subs: 2931 E. McCarty St., P.O. Box 3710, Jefferson City, MO
   65102
Monthly during school year (see below)
$3.90; $1.95 each for 10 or more subscriptions to same address

First graders make up the target audience of this four-page weekly. Illustrations are clear and colorful; text is kept simple for beginning readers. The front page is consistently inviting. The four issues of a month are mailed at one time.

Within one particular three-month period, first graders are introduced to presidents and inventors, collectors, poetry by black Americans, hydroponically grown vegetables, nests, teeth, and the artwork of Navajo children. One issue is meant to be cut to form a little book containing an Eskimo folktale. Each month, a colorful calendar on the last page of one issue advises of special days and celebrations and asks the child about this and that (Do you like oatmeal?) or suggests that the child do something (Draw a butterfly in the next box.). In the other three issues, the back page might carry simple word exercises for the child to complete or leave space for items to be drawn.

The format of the weekly is quite attractive and should engage the interest of many young children. Layout is uncluttered, and background no longer competes with text. Drawings and photographs, with a few exceptions, are reproduced exceedingly well. Words for the child to read are printed especially clearly; choice of typeface and use of space aid clarity. The vocabulary is such that there are words the child will be able to identify and decode, as well as a few that will be challenging.

The edition for teachers ($19 subscription for the school year; free with 10 or more subscriptions of the child's edition) includes a copy of the child's magazine and might be of interest to parents wanting or able to guide their offspring's reading, particularly if the magazine is not being ordered for the child through a classroom. For the articles on each page of the child's edition, background information, discussion questions, activities, and sometimes book suggestions are provided, all of which extend and enrich the use of the magazine.

Scholastic News: Ranger
Scholastic Inc.
Edit: 730 Broadway, New York, NY 10003
Subs: 2931 E. McCarty St., P.O. Box 3710, Jefferson City, MO
   65102
Weekly during school year (26 issues)
$3.90; $1.95 each for 10 or more subscriptions to same address

Primarily for second graders, the weekly *Ranger* continues the four-page 8-by-10⅞-inch format of the newsprint *Pilot*. The reading level is upgraded by using more difficult words and longer sentences and paragraphs. Color is an integral part of content and used appropriately. Standards for legibility of print are maintained, and layout is attractive and well composed. Photographs are likely to feature children the same age as the readers. Diagrams are clearly and carefully drawn. From issues received for review, it appears that some issues in a month are given precise dates, while others are marked week one, week two, and so forth. To the regular pages are occasionally added supplements—for example, about family sharing and animals. Exercises, tips, and questions for thought might be found on pages other than the first one.

Three issues, in one month examined, continue the cover story on the center pages. "A Law to Help Disabled Americans" is followed by brief paragraphs about new technologies for the hearing and seeing impaired. "Cleaning Up the Air" precedes a double-page drawing of the sources of air pollution and some experiments. A full-color cover photograph of the start of a dogsled race leads into an interview with a man who has won four times. The last page of this issue carries a "News Review" (fill in the blanks) and a Peanuts cartoon. The fourth issue of this particular month brings an Eskimo folktale that appeared in *Pilot*, with the same illustrations and only slight changes in the wording. In other issues too, the same content is presented; illustrations sometimes are and sometimes are not different. Adjustments are made in readability levels, that is, in vocabulary and sentence length.

The edition for teachers carries background notes and ideas for extending the content of an issue. "Facts Behind the Headlines" is a caption frequently used.

Scholastic News: Trails
Scholastic Inc.
Edit: 730 Broadway, New York, NY 10003
Subs: 2931 E. McCarty St., P.O. Box 3710, Jefferson City, MO 65102
Weekly during school year (26 issues)
$4.50; $2.25 each for 10 or more subscriptions to same address
Ranger leads to *Trails*, suggested for third graders. The amount of textual material is increased, but heed is still given to pictorial matter, especially photographs and simple drawings and diagrams. The four-page newsprint weekly is readily recognized as an "older" member of the *News* family that has its beginnings in *Pilot*.

A March issue carries reports not unlike the features of the editions for younger children. The cover story is headlined "Law Would Help Disabled Americans." The headline is developed in three paragraphs on the cover page. Inside on page two are two related stories about people with disabilities. One speaks of a computer that reads to the blind; a black-and-white photograph shows a woman using the scanner. The other report is about a dog that helps a handicapped child. Page three includes a three-paragraph account of a dogsled race, a map of the route, and an interview with a winning racer. All the subjects of the three pages are covered in other editions too. As with the newsmagazines for other grades, one issue a month of *Scholastic Newstime* presents a monthly calendar on the last page. The

specific items listed on the calendar, however, differ, and the monthly celebrations (National Nutrition Month, for instance) are not the same as in
editions for younger children.

Word and math puzzles, as well as other activities, challenge the
reader. "News and Vocabulary Review" tests some of the learnings of the
issue. Boxes captioned "Words to Know" located alongside articles give
help with definitions. Full color is used on most pages. Occasionally, the
center pages are highlighted with a single color. Photographs and drawings continue to be used as illustrations, with an edge given to photographs in issues examined.

An edition is available for teachers, as is true of the other titles in the
series.

Scholastic Newstime
  Scholastic Inc.
  Edit: 730 Broadway, New York, NY 10003
  Subs: 2931 E. McCarty St., P.O. Box 3710, Jefferson City, MO
    65102
  Weekly during school year (26 issues)
  $5.00; $2.50 each for 10 or more subscriptions to same address
The top of the line of *Scholastic* newsmagazines for elementary grades,
Newstime for sixth graders is the last step before students switch to the
venerable *Junior Scholastic*. Of tabloid size, as *Citizen* for fifth graders,
Newstime contains content similar to that found in the four-page weeklies.
Text of like articles is sometimes very similar and other times somewhat
altered. The same illustrations might be used, although size might be
changed. However, the locations of articles and illustrations in *Citizen* and
Newstime are usually shuffled, thus giving a change in emphasis. *Newstime's* back page carries at the top, in three issues examined, the same
"Almanac" as in *Citizen* and at the bottom, skills similar in format. Full
color is used on the outside pages; a touch of color is added to inside pages.
Photographs are the main form of illustration.

The front-page coverage of the situation in South Africa aptly encapsulates the viewpoints and events in 11 well-written paragraphs. The com-
plexities and issues of the situation are cast in language an average sixth
grader could read without losing the importance and seriousness of the
troubles. The pronunciation for *apartheid* is given in parens, and the word
is defined in context. Quotes from key figures reveal the dilemmas. From
the brief report, children can grasp the essentials of this news and, in addition, could develop some thoughts about the elements of crisp and clear
newswriting. Underscoring the intent of the weekly to cover world news,
the story under the lead one is about the concern over the use of fishing
nets in international waters. The column at the right briefly reports on
both a high school girl who is kicker for a football team and some upcoming
television specials.

The monthly "Almanac" of the back page prints squibs on history, government, sports, inventions, holidays and celebrations, food, health, and
"firsts," accompanied by colorful drawings. The exercises at the bottom

also take on an international flavor with questions about the geography and history of foreign countries. A "News and Vocabulary Review" asks readers to distinguish between fact and opinion. (Even adults can learn of the tug of personal opinion in responding to such items as "drift nets should be banned in all countries.")

The newsmagazine is well worth the price of a single subscription when the title is not made available in the classroom. The content addresses matters of which an informed citizenry should be aware. Through this basic magazine, children can be introduced to current affairs. The edition for teachers is similar in content and format to guides for the magazines for younger students; however, a slight upgrading in the difficulty of activities and quizzes can be noted.

Scholastic Sprint
   Scholastic Inc.
   Edit: 730 Broadway, New York, NY 10003
   Subs: 2931 E. McCarty St., P.O. Box 3710, Jefferson City, MO
      65102
   Biweekly during school year: September–April (14 issues)
   $12; $5.95 each for 10 or more subscriptions to same address
Prepared especially for students in fourth through sixth grade who are reading on second- and third-grade levels, the biweekly is the same size, 8 by 10⅞ inches, as other Scholastic elementary school classroom newspapers, but this one runs to 16 pages. Apparently, to be sure to hook readers, care is given to arrangement of pages so that, although busy, they are not crowded or forbidding. The intent is to offer an integrated approach to the development of basic language-arts skills for students with special learning needs. The colorful newsprint magazine manages to present subject matter of interest to children, as well as entertaining activities, within a limited vocabulary. The print is large and clear; articles are supplemented by pictures and drawings.

A colorful and upbeat cover is followed by "News Watch," with brief reports and an exercise. In three issues examined, a five-page play of many scenes (two based on books) is the first major feature. A page of puzzles precedes the next two two-page articles or stories. Among the subjects of the articles are the census, animal camouflage, a major league star, and American Indian dancers. The fiction has offered both a brief story with a contemporary setting and a folktale. "The B Team" (J.R., Linda, and Richard Busby) portrays in five boxed photographs the need for consumer or study skills. The adjacent page provides exercises related to the specific skill. The back page, "Eye Opener," makes use of vocabulary in the issue in identifying a mystery photo.

An edition for teachers is available that reviews vocabulary and suggests new words to teach, as well as enumerates questions for discussion. Some youngsters just might want to enjoy the magazine for its own sake. One can only hope a teacher doesn't overkill by being thorough with the guide. A subscription to the edition for teachers is free with bulk orders and can be ordered separately at $20; the price includes a copy of *Sprint*.

School Mates
U.S. Chess Federation
186 Route 9W, New Windsor, NY 12553
Quarterly; $7.50

Intended for beginning chess players of any age but "probably best suited to under twenty," the quarterly represents children well in its black-and-white photographs. The main attraction for regular readers might be the tactics or strategies outlined. Articles, when not about particular tournaments or games, provide reports about people, ranging from champions to families that enjoy the game. Other articles spotlight chess in early America and tell how to use a chess clock. Regularly appearing pages are "Winning Chess Tactics," "Test Your Tactics," and "Tournaments Designed with YOU in Mind," which lists events by state. Issues usually report the plays of some championship games.

In one issue, the All-American Chess Team, an annual selection recognizing young players, is announced. The 43 members are shown individually in a head shot, along with indications of school subjects (presumably favorites or ones in which they excel), interests, and career goals. The boys far outnumber the girls; however, the youngest player, age six, is a girl. "Readers Write" is the regular letters-to-the-editor page, which often corrects mistakes in previous issues. The magazine's cover typically presents a black-and-white photograph of a champion, but drawings have also appeared there. A single touch of color is added to most of the 8½-by-11-inch pages; sometimes the color is limited to the words in a title. The many diagrams of chess boards on the 20 pages of an issue probably supply the illustrations most appreciated by players.

Although the chess illiterate probably won't be able to handle the strategies, this quarterly, "The U.S. Chess Federation's Magazine for Young Chessplayers," has some material for browsing or for luring new recruits to the game. Certainly those youngsters who play chess will be interested in subscriptions.

Science World
Scholastic Inc.
Edit: 730 Broadway, New York, NY 10003
Subs: 2931 E. McCarty St., P.O. Box 3710, Jefferson City, MO
　　　65102
Biweekly during school year (18 issues)
$9.50; $5.95 each for 10 or more subscriptions to same address

Like most Scholastic educational publications, this magazine lures the reader with a lively format and manages to present facts and concepts while providing an update on science in today's world. Among the captions used for articles are the following: "Life Science," "Earth Science," "Health/Medicine," "Environment," "Astronomy/Space Science," and "Physical Science/Technology." This biweekly for grades 7 to 10 is meant to help develop thinking and research skills and a science vocabulary. The well-written and informative articles should enable the intended audience to do so.

The contents page lists the reports and short pieces under "Features" or "Departments." The number of features in an issue varies, with as many as six in one issue. Among recent cover stories are those about twins (including the scientists' studying of nature and nuture) and the issues involved when deer and people seek the same living space. Other articles discuss "Why Buildings Don't Sink" (David Macaulay), AIDS, and chemical fertilizers and pesticides. Names of authors are given with the titles; the assistant editor contributes quite a few. Among the regular departments toward the back of an issue are "Crossword" and "The Far Side," a cartoon by Gary Larson. Other items under "Departments" present experiments, profiles, and trivia. Brief news items related to the sciences are reported under "Currents."

Full-color photographs and original drawings, as well as charts, tables, graphs, and maps, enhance each 24-page issue. About two-thirds of the photographs in an issue are black and white. The cover full-color photograph succeeds in making its own point.

The magazine will probably not be of great interest to children below fifth or sixth grade, but it is one of several science magazines that children in upper elementary grades and junior high should be exposed to in order to indicate preferences regarding subscriptions, whether for classroom, library, or home.   *Children's Magazine Guide*

Scienceland
501 Fifth Ave., Suite 2108, New York, NY 10017
Monthly during school year: September–May; except December (8 issues)

$15.95, regular edition; $36, deluxe edition

The target audience for this 26-page science monthly is kindergarten through grade three; however, children beyond either end of the span are also likely to be enthralled by the full-color photographs on the 8¼-by-11¾-inch glossy pages. The magazine's intent, "To Nurture Scientific Thinking," is recorded on the cover. Most issues center on a very specific topic—for example, ants, icicles, or rubber. The color photographs come in different sizes, never allowing the highly pictorial layout to become tiresome or predictable. Colorful close-up photographs make many subjects vivid. The publication is like a magazine insofar as it is published monthly and has a special subject interest, although it is unlike many periodicals in that there are no regular columns, contents pages (there is a brief table of contents on the back cover), or reader contributions. Promotional material states that the publication is designed and edited like a book. The contents of the regular and deluxe editions are identical; however, the deluxe edition is printed on very heavy coated paper, and the regular edition is printed on lighter stock, glossy and heavier than newsprint.

One issue, but not a typical one, carries a special report entitled "Journey to the Amazon." The front cover pictures the largest beetle in the world (the photographed one is even larger than life size) and the back cover, a pygmy marmoset on the arm of a boy. Between the covers are pictured the Amazon River and the jungle and the fish, insects, fruits, flowers, boats, and children of the area. More typical is the issue "All about Pinecones!", which pictures the life cycle of the pine tree and suggests an experiment and crafts using the cones. Other issues have focused on cats, chipmunks, cheetahs, crayfish, sloths, snow, strawberries, hands, hermit crabs, pond life, and robots. Some back issues continue to be available from the publisher. The science of *Scienceland* is primarily biology; by and large, the content deals primarily with animals, followed by plants and, then by people or human anatomy.

At the end of each issue, a vocabulary list provides pronunciations and definitions. Several pages suggest activities requiring close observation or visual discrimination. Questions to the reader are interspersed with factual information. Large print and short sentences are meant to make the text manageable for young readers. Notes in smaller print are intended for readers beyond the beginning stages and adults using the magazine with children. Text is usually printed distinctly; occasionally, the words fall on dark backgrounds.

The large-scale format of the magazine, curiously, suggests an immediacy and intimacy with regard to its topics. There is little to distract from the subject of the large pictures. Many color photographs equal the work of some other nature magazines, although the photographers aren't usually identified. Color drawings too are well executed. The publication is visually impressive. All three recent issues sent for review, however, point to a problem with printing. The dramatic effect that might have been conveyed in double-page spreads is diminished by the vertical white line of the gutter.

There is a peculiarity in the numbering of pages; odd numbers are on the left side. Issues are identified on the cover by volume and a sequential number dating to the first issue in 1977. (Volume 13, number 101 is the October 1989 issue.)

A monthly, 28-page booklet for teachers (or parents) is available at $12 a year. The guide contains background information, discussion questions, projects and activities, an introduction to the issue, and a list of objectives.

Children's Magazine Guide

Seedling Series: Short Story International
International Cultural Exchange
6 Sheffield Rd., Great Neck, NY 11021
Quarterly; $14

A 64-page quarterly reprinting seven or eight stories in each issue, *Seedling Series* seeks to give an international flavor to the reading material of children in grades four to seven. On the contents page, the countries from which the stories come or in which they are set are clearly designated at the left margin in alphabetic order by country. The stories are primarily from magazines and books, although the authors retain copyright for some. Folktales are among the stories presented. For each story, there is at least one full-page illustration at the beginning; sometimes a second drawing is placed within the story. Because all the artwork is by one or two illustrators, there is little suggestion of the diversity in cultures and lifestyles of the world. The 5¼-by-8¼-inch magazine announces on its cover that it brings "exciting tales from all over the world."

In the issue sent for examination, the seven stories listed represent six countries. Because there is no biographical information about the authors, it cannot be determined whether they are from the countries named, although several of the names suggest an association with the countries listed. The countries represented are Japan, Nepal, Scotland, the United States (two stories), the USSR, and Vietnam. Although an intent of the content is to give children "insight into the cultures and lifestyles of people from all over the globe," save for two contributions, a non-American setting is not integral to the stories.

The first story seems to be Japanese by virtue only of the names of the family members. "A Sunday Fight," about squabbling, is told from the point of view of the mother. It is startling to read in the first line of a children's story "my husband," but even allowing the author a chance to try a twist, the incessant dialogue fails to captivate. The second story (not a short story in the literary sense) is a brief account of the mysterious yeti of the Himalayas, or the search for the Abominable Snowman. The third story, the longest by far at 20 pages, first appeared in *Dragon*. "Eira" is set in a fantasy kingdom and is about the young bard Derwen, a female harpist who overcomes the evil of Eira's cold world. The first of the two stories from the United States is about Johnny Maple planting seedlings; "Johnny's Arbor Day Project" is reprinted from *Grit*. In the second, "The Renaming of Small Girl," the protagonist is a native American. The tribe is not named, but the setting is near "the thundering falls that were called Niagara." The story from the USSR, "The Happiest Day," is the first-person account of a boy's manipulations to bring back together his quarreling parents. With a setting in Vietnam, "The Two-Steps Snake" is the tale of a boy and his cousin who harbor some snakes so lethal that two steps after being bitten, the victim dies.

Issues may be purchased separately for $4.45. The publisher also prepares a quarterly for grades 8 through 12, *Student Series: Short Story International*.

Senior Weekly Reader see *Weekly Reader Senior Edition*

Sesame Street Magazine
    Children's Television Workshop
    Edit: One Lincoln Plaza, New York, NY 10023
    Subs: P.O. Box 55518, Boulder, CO 80322
    Monthly; except February and August (10 issues)
    $13.97

A colorful magazine for preschoolers, this monthly published since 1971 seems to show no decline; rather, the editors continue to polish their fare. The magazine is a fine introduction to certain characteristics of magazines, including diversity in content of an issue and consistency from issue to issue. The publisher successfully responds to the interests and abilities of its targeted audience, children two to six. This jolly magazine is filled with games, puzzles, activities, picture stories, and verses—content that will help children become, quite painlessly, proficient in such skills as naming letters of the alphabet, matching objects, reading pictures, identifying shapes, recognizing colors, working with numbers, telling time, and listening to poems and stories. The full-color artwork is particularly suitable for young children, showing a variety of styles in each issue; and the illustrators are important enough to the publication to be identified. The magazine format, because it can be heterogeneous, offers a fitting way to introduce the young to many styles and media of illustration. (Some magazines never seem to go much beyond cartoon-like drawings.)

On the contents page, the titles of the pieces within are placed under "Stories and Poems" or "Games and Activities." The former usually has about five entries and the latter, 10 or more. Under the titles, the skills that are addressed are specified for the adult. Each issue centers on a theme, an important one in the world of the young child. Within one year, the magazine featured sound; up and down; silliness; growing up; emotions; land, sea, and sky; back to school; signs and symbols; food; and holidays. Themes are carried out exceedingly well. The characters of the television program regularly make appearances. Cookie Monster, Big Bird, and the rest of the gang are readily recognized in the 32 pages of the monthly. The layout of the 8⅛-by-10¾-inch pages suggests that particular attention has been given to the arranging of the elements, for practical and aesthetic reasons. Pages always appear lively but never cluttered. Full color is used throughout. The centerfold always brings a poster.

An examination of the issue about night and day should suggest ways that the editors cleverly develop a theme and consistently present features a notch above those typical of some other publishers. The content, informative and instructive, is also delightfully humorous and upbeat. The child is urged (the second person is used throughout) to think further about whatever is pictured on the pages through questions unlike workbook exercises. The front cover, under a "Good Morning" greeting, pictures smiling Ernie waking to a sunny day; the back cover shows contented (and smiling) Grover cuddled in the arms of the reader of his bedtime story, a happy conclusion to the content of the issue. The last picture also hides numerous stars for the child to find, some bearing smiles.

Inside the front cover, a snapshot from the Sesame Street family album introduces Hoots the Owl, who likes to stay up at night playing his saxophone. The child is asked what he or she does all day and what he or she does at night. The listing of the content, in small print and obviously for the adult, places the inner matter under "Stories and Poems," of which there are three, and "Games and Activities," numbering about 15. Under each title of the contents page is noted the learning activity—comparing pictures, for example. The page announces that the featured letters in the issue are "M" and "N" and that the special number is "7." Inside, there are two lively, even zany, full-page illustrations in which the child is to find objects that begin with "M" or "N." In one, the observer will find a monkey wearing mittens riding a motorcycle, a mermaid admiring herself in a mirror, and much more. In the other, each member of a chorus line of nine

Ns waves an object beginning with the letter. This picture, appropriately, will be slightly more challenging for some; for example, the child might or might not discover the carrot nose. For both letters, the young one is urged to think of other words that begin with these letters.

In the double-page spread "The Count Counts Constellations," the Draculan vampire of lilac-colored face, fanged teeth, triangular nose, and broad grin peers through a telescope to find the North Star and thereby the seven stars of the little dipper. The outlines of both dippers and bears can be readily seen by holding the page up to a light. In a brief paragraph, the child is introduced to the meaning of the word *constellation* and to the Latin names for the bears. (Many children will find these words delicious; the magazine is to be praised for not shying away from them.)

The initial story in the same issue is a four-page, eight-box picture tale titled "From Morning to Night with Grover." Grover is to be cut out from the side of one page and inserted in the slot of each colorful drawing as he moves through the activities of his happy day. The other story of this particular issue is a photo essay—full-color photographs of Stephen accompanying his mother to her office. Mother is a black woman who carries a briefcase. The poetry feature, printed on both sides of one sheet, is meant to be pulled out and folded to form a little book of nighttime poems.

Among the games and activities in the night-and-day issue is a simple version of a board game captioned "Wake Up!" The inhabitants of a house, on one page, and of a forest, on another, are sleeping, save for an owl and one cat. The two illustrations become the boards. Squares picturing the people and animals awakening are to be cut out and placed over their sleeping counterparts. Not a simple matching game, although it could be used for that purpose only, this game requires a paper bag from which the two players draw the squares. If the square doesn't match the scene on the person's board, back it goes into the bag. Further on, adjacent pages, noteworthy for the clarity of the full-page illustrations (some objects seemingly cut out of paper), show a smiling sun and sleepy moon in the top left corners. The child is to find objects that might be associated with each—an egg sunny-side up, for example.

The centerfold is a poster with a bedtime checklist captioned "Sweet Dreams, Ernie." After the center pages are pulled out of the magazine, the two visible pages reveal another morning-night exercise. Bert, Ernie, and Oscar begin their day on the left, descending the stairs of a crosscut of their house, and end their day on the right. Careful scrutiny of the pictures will suggest some of the things the threesome did during the day; in addition, children can note differences between the two pictures.

A feature about sign language appears regularly; in this issue, Linda shows in full-color photographs how to say good morning and good night, as well as "I'm tired" and "I'm hungry." In "Morning on the Farm," a double-page spread of a farmyard, eight animals and their sounds are introduced. The cutouts on the edges of the pages are to be placed in the appropriate abodes. The names of the animals are also given in Spanish, along with a pronunciation guide. A calendar for the month allows room for the child to write in any upcoming special plans or events. Holidays are marked with little illustrations; the child is instructed to mark off each day as it passes. A few pages later, instructions are printed for making a paper lantern, an object significant to one of the holidays. On the regular "Readers' Pages" are poems, pictures, and riddles submitted by subscribers.

This is a magazine meant to be demolished (cut, marked, colored, and so on), and therefore, a personal subscription is most desirable. Nevertheless, libraries too need subscriptions. Librarians can alert parents to the qualities of the magazine, some of which aren't necessarily obvious on first glance. Librarians and teachers can offer advice to other adults about how the monthly can be used to help children develop skills—joyfully. An ad for the magazine claims it will help children learn about colors, shapes, letters, and numbers and will foster thinking, creativity, and problem solving. *Sesame Street* certainly has the potential to do all that. The magazine continues to reign as the best of the general-interest magazines for young children.

A subscription includes two sections: the issue for children and *Parent's Guide*, which is really a magazine in its own right, running to over 30 pages. Only a few pages directly correlate with the content of *Sesame Street Magazine*. Two pages about the night-and-day issue (discussed above) suggest ways to extend the content of the child's magazine. The basic concepts dealt with in the theme are discussed, and specific activities are suggested to help the child grasp the rhythms in the passage of day and night and the phases of the moon. The second page recommends children's books and audio tapes about the theme.

Children's Magazine Guide

Shoe Tree
> **National Association for Young Writers**
> Edit: 215 Valle del Sol Dr., Santa Fe, NM 87501
> Subs: P.O. Box 3000, Dept. YW, Denville, NJ 07834
> 3 issues: Fall, Winter, and Spring/Summer
> $15

This "little" magazine for children adheres to high standards of writing and production. "The Literary Magazine by and for Young Writers" welcomes stories, poems, and artwork from children ages 6 to 14. Book reviews are also published. On the contents page, the fiction and nonfiction are listed separately, with poetry usually falling between the two, although all are intermingled within the 64 pages of this 6-by-9-inch magazine. The full-color cover illustration, quite different from issue to issue, is the work of children too. The prose and poetry read exceedingly well. Children, whether writers or not, should derive pleasure from reading about the real and imagined experiences of their peers. A dash of humor adds spice to many entries.

A recent issue's full-color cover presents an exquisite drawing about the visions of an old wise man's mind, a work that had been shown in a Navajo children's art show. The poem, "Shoe Tree," is always printed on the first page, with an illustration of a girl reading at the base of a tree and a boy dangling from an upper limb. Within this issue are six fiction stories, a dozen poems, one nonfiction story, and two book reviews. In addition to the illustrations accompanying one story, two fine works, a moose and a wolf, by Santa Fe youths are shown in black and white. An author of children's books gives suggestions for overcoming writer's block.

First place in this same issue is given to the first-prize winner of the poetry contest and second place, to the second-prize winner. The first, "Black," by a 10-year-old, goes much beyond the more typical black-is-an-object lines to suggest sounds and textures and ends with the thought, "Black is midnight, the fulfillment of dark." The remaining 10 poems received honorable mention in the contest. Most of the poems are rich in imagery, seemingly the work of precocious children. Strong emotions, particularly about fears and death, are poignantly conveyed in nearly half of the poems. Only one poem could really be called humorous. The staff is to be commended for attracting and publishing poems of such quality. Four of the half dozen fiction stories in the issue are by 10-year-olds. The stories show much variety in subject, thought, and style. One of the brief stories sensitively tells of the morning after in Hiroshima, and another amusingly relates the foiled plans to get a pet dog. In all six stories, the child's voice prevails. The two-page nonfiction story is titled "What Can We Do to Help Wolves?"

Toward the back of each issue is an article of encouragement and advice to would-be writers by a published (adult) author. The three-page "Author to Author" feature has told of "Writing with Voice" and "A Writer's Hidden Power" (to make readers laugh and cry and experience other emotions). Also in the final pages, contributors are accorded biographical listings that include their interests other than writing. Children who want to illustrate the work of others and to write book reviews are advised to indicate their interests to the editor.

In addition to regular submissions, each issue runs a competition. The entries for the fiction contest of the Spring issue may be short stories, parts of novels, or plays. The poetry contest for the Fall issue accepts serious and humorous work but no haiku, cinquain, or classrooom assignments. For the nonfiction competition of the Winter issue, narrative essays or feature articles may be submitted.

The title of the magazine comes from a legend about an old oak tree under which, in early days, barefoot country folk met to exchange stories with neighbors before putting on their shoes to attend worship services across the village green. The editors conceived the magazine "as a kind of meeting place, a spot to sit and while away the hours with friends or with one's own imagination . . . to exchange stories and ideas." Sheila Cowing has been editor-in-chief since 1987. The magazine was first published two years earlier.

The layout of the pages suggests an understanding of restrained and respectful, if not dignified, ways to present the writing of the young. The paper is of good quality and the covers of sturdy tagboard. Typeface is clear and legible and, therefore, easily read. Sufficient white space allows for an uncluttered appearance of print and illustration.

The editors hope that their publication will stimulate writing. That it seems to be doing. Not to be overlooked is the value to writing of reading the work of others. This magazine affords children the opportunity to read other children's creative stories and poems, imaginative writings showing great diversity in writing styles.

Short Story International see *Seedling Series*

Skipping Stones
   Aprovecho Institute
   80574 Hazelton Rd., Cottage Grove, OR 97424
   Quarterly; $15

The aims of this small press quarterly are "to encourage cooperation, creativity and celebration of cultural and linguistic diversity" and "to explore and to learn stewardship of the ecological web that sustains us." The two emphases are mingled in the content; a worldwide perspective is evident for both. A black-and-white photograph on the cover usually introduces the major story. The remaining pages are filled with brief items, some with page captions. As indicated in the subtitle, "A Multi-ethnic Children's Forum," many of the submissions are from children, and quite a few of these young people reside outside the United States. The 8½-by-11-inch pages are filled but not cluttered with text and illustration, mostly black-and-white photographs and drawings. The 32 pages are printed on recycled paper. Meant by the publisher for children up to 14 years of age, children under six are probably not really in the targeted audience of the magazine.

Cover stories in recent issues center on environmental awareness, Ethiopia, and images of India. A bilingual issue features Mexico and Central America. Life and customs in third-world countries are portrayed, along with holidays and celebrations, in articles, stories, and photo essays. Games, songs, crafts, maps, and calendars round out an issue. Children are urged to submit stories, reports, poems, letters, reviews, games (cooperative), instructions for making things, recipes, puzzles, riddles, photographs, and drawings, and this material is to be found in most issues. Submissions are welcome in all languages.

Among captions to pages that appear with seeming regularity is "Cultural Collage," a miscellany of contributions from young people of Oregon and elsewhere. (The captioning does not make clear whether this is one page in length or extends over several pages to the next regularly appearing caption.) "Skipping Stones Stew" reprints brief submissions, primarily verses, from U.S. children and children abroad. "Networking" briefly reports activities of associations (including sponsors of the magazine) and clubs (including those of children) in this country and other countries, activities in keeping with the intent of the quarterly. Other events and projects reported by readers find place in "Noteworthy N.E.W.S." (*n*orth, *e*ast, *w*est, *s*outh). In "Books to Look For," titles pertinent to the magazine's aims are noted; in addition to books from major trade publishers, some from small presses and educational publishers are suggested. A letter or two appear in "Pen Pals," along with names and addresses of those seeking correspondents. "Want to Fiddle with These Riddles?" brings puzzlements from around the world, while "Some Things You Might Do or Share" often nurtures word play in non-English languages.

The intent of the magazine is to provide a place for children of diverse backgrounds to share their experiences. The goal is to reach children all over the world, "in economically disadvantaged as well as privileged families, including underrepresented and special populations within North America." To this end, free copies are sent to schools and libraries in the third world and low-income ones in the United States.

Sports Illustrated for Kids
The Time Inc. Magazine Co.
Edit: Time & Life Bldg., Rockefeller Center, New York, NY 10020
Subs: P.O. Box 830609, Birmingham, AL 35283
Monthly
$15.95; $10.95 each for 10 or more subscriptions to same address

The excitement and tension of sports are captured in the action-filled full-color photographs and brisk writing of this energetic monthly of some 90 pages. Intended for girls and boys ages 8 to 13 (and aiming at a fifth-grade reading level), the magazine carries much material about professional sports, but young people also are featured. Most issues bring four major articles and a dozen regular departments. Photography and graphics are highly professional and polished. Full color is used on all pages, including the 20 or so bearing ads in an issue. The focus of the 8⅛-by-10⅞-inch magazine is on fun, but stories "emphasize the importance of values such as hard work, teamwork, practice, fair play, and a positive attitude." Baseball, basketball, football, hockey, track, and gymnastics are sure to be covered in a highly pictorial way in a year's subscription.

"Quick Kicks," a regular column, gives a roundup of news from the sports world. The feature articles sometimes cover professional sports but are more likely to be about children. In one issue of four articles, the cover story is about two young boys who race quarter-midget cars, and another article profiles an 18-year-old girl, winner of major tennis tournaments. "Games Kids Play" centers on discs and describes a few spins for Frisbee players to try. "Kids Take Over," which has also appeared as a regular department, in this issue follows an eighth grader who was commissioned to take photographs at an all-star game. In other issues, the major articles have covered young skiers, snowboarding, cheerleading, early World Series games, professional soccer, and three youngsters who went to the White House to check out the sports facilities. Most articles are four to six pages in length, with much of this space filled with photographs of high quality.

Among the regularly appearing columns, some are seasonal, some come and go, some are about young people in sports, some contain biographies of pros and their playing tips, and some are stories and puzzles for amusement. On a cork board are posted "Letters" from readers about their interests in sports and the magazine, and usually three color snapshots. "Hotshots" profiles young athletes who are "getting the most out of sports," often meaning that they are excelling. A young member of a pro's family is featured in "Home Team," along with the relationship to the star. Children interview a prominent player in "Press Conference." Of the biographical pieces, the one that dips into history is "Legends," which has recalled Jim Thorpe and Jesse Owens. "Tips from the Pros" offers advice, and "My Worst Day" reveals mistakes and hard times in sports. In "Ask Dr. Psych," a sports psychologist deals with such things as the mind sets that can improve the score, and learning to relax under pressure.

For collectors, there are "Sports Cards," nine on a page for punching out, and the centerspread poster, which is folded in quarters. Readers are asked to take the role of referee in "What's the Call?", where answers require knowledge of rules. A miscellany of word puzzles, matching items, identifying differences, and board games is found toward the end of an issue in "Play-by-Play." Even the most overtested child probably won't object to the multiple-choice questions on the baseball aptitude test. Four-page fiction stories with sports connections are printed in "Jack B. Quick," who is a detective, and "Professor Fleet," the owner of a fabulous adventure appliance. And at the very end of an issue is "Buzz Beamer," a cartoon strip.

Certain to be tattered after a few days on a library shelf, this monthly almost stands alone in an area where other publishers have not succeeded in holding ground for long. A guide for teachers, "Chalk Talk," is free with bulk orders. Each month 250,000 copies of the magazine are donated to schools attended by children at risk.   *Children's Magazine Guide*

Sprint see *Scholastic Sprint*

Stone Soup
Children's Art Foundation
P.O. Box 83, Santa Cruz, CA 95063
5 issues a year: September, November, January, March, and May
$22

"The Magazine by Children" announces the subtitle, and all the stories, poems, book reviews, and art within the 48-page issues *are* contributed by children through age 13. To initiate a literary magazine for and by children, one that will publish only the best of the submissions, is not for the lily-livered. Since 1973, editors Gerry Mandel and William Rubel have been dedicated to encouraging children to write and to aim for quality in their work. The writing that appears reflects the imagination and interests of creative children. The artwork on the front cover, printed in full color, is always by children. Within the issues are many black-and-white drawings and photographs, along with four pages of art in full color. Paper of high quality, a particularly clear typeface, and heedful spacing of material add to the substantial nature of this 6-by-8¾-inch magazine—a little magazine with great respect for the writing of children. The authors, poets, painters, illustrators, and reviewers are accorded full acknowledgment for their contributions. A black-and-white photograph of the contributor accompanies the person's name, age, and home town. An annual index is published in the May issue.

In one issue examined, seven stories are published. In all of them, the child voice is evident, yet all read very smoothly. The initial story, a first-person account by a native American girl, relates the perils of herding sheep in New Mexico. The second story shares the author's feelings at the time her horse died. Stories by two recent immigrants tell of life in Cambodia versus life in the United States. Another story captures in a few pages the tensions between pitcher and catcher that led to a game loss. The youngest author, 10 years old, writes of a boy fascinated by a spider making a web, a spider that falls prey to a cat. One of the longer stories, notable for its characterization of the protagonist, recalls a babysitting experience that went awry because of some irresponsible decisions. Certainly, the stories in toto, though not wildly upbeat, deal with feelings and emotions familiar to the young. Five of the authors are 12 or 13; about half of the stories are illustrated by their authors. Two of the stories are seven pages long, but the average length is around three pages.

Five poems are printed in this same issue. Two by a 10-year-old boy were prompted by the playground slayings in Stockton. The poems published suggest that the editorial weeding process is thorough. Jingles and doggerel do not make it to these pages. Two book reviews, one two pages in length, evaluate recent titles from major publishers. Drawings made with color pencils illustrate two stories. Book reviews and illustrations for stories are usually assigned to children who express an interest in doing this type of work. Two gouache paintings on adjacent pages of a yacht harbor came out of a summer painting class. This particular artwork allows for an interesting study of similarities and differences.

At the center of every issue is a two-page guide that discusses the issue's stories and pictures, drawing attention to noteworthy elements and suggesting projects young writers and artists might try. The insert, on tinted paper, is meant to be used by children on their own (or as an aid to classroom teachers). While the aforementioned "Activities" should prove helpful to the young, would-be writers ought to consider "Information for Contributors" near the front of each issue. The suggestions are succinct and pertinent and could give direction to children, whether planning to make submissions or not. The editors prefer to receive writing and art based on personal experiences and observations. "If you feel strongly about something that happened to you or something you observed, use that feeling as a basis for your story, poem, or picture." A story should have a clear beginning, middle, and ending and also have a point to make. Dialogue should sound like real people talking. Characters, places, sounds, and smells can be made vivid by use of detail. About poems, the advice is, "Choose your words carefully! When your poem is read aloud, the words should sound beautiful and rhythmical, almost like music." Thus, the criteria for selection are spelled out and also serve to describe the magazine's output. How very different this magazine from publications that are the vanity press of the child market!

The publisher, the Children's Art Foundation, is a nonprofit orfaniza-
tion that also operates the Museum of Children's Art and the Children's
Art School. The artwork of the magazine's cover and of the color pages
within usually comes from these institutions. The Museum collects art by
children from around the world. The publishing of such work gives a
delightful international flavor to the magazine. And yes, the work is of
"museum quality." Books, T-shirts, note cards, and postcards are also
available from the Foundation.

Summer Weekly Reader see *Weekly Reader*

SuperScience
Scholastic Inc.
Edit: P.O. Box 3710, 730 Broadway, New York, NY 10003
Subs: 2931 E. McCarty St., Jefferson City, MO 65102
Monthly during school year: September–May, except bimonthly
  November/December (8 issues)
$7.90; $3.95 each for 10 or more subscriptions to same address;
  Red edition
$9.50; $4.75 each for 10 or more subscriptions to same address;
  Blue edition

A classroom periodical about science, this monthly was introduced by
Scholastic in 1989. Published in two editions, and levels of difficulty,
SuperScience Red is meant for grades one to three, and *Blue* is for grades
four to six. Both editions are highly pictorial—in color and inviting. Both
are the same size, 8 by 10⅞ inches; however, the one for younger children
has 16 pages and the edition for older children, twice as many. The publication is a "mass media project" funded in part by the National Science
Foundation. The *Red* edition is described first below.

Issues of the edition for lower grades take a theme for focus and
approach the subject with hands-on lessons and activities. In carrying out
the theme, the emphasis is on doing. Action, or the verb, is stressed rather
than the object, or the noun. For example, an issue is about seeing rather
than eyes. The intent is to involve children in experimenting; they are
kept busy gathering evidence and recording observations. A project is usually shown on a double-page spread, a fitting format for the instructions
and tasks.

A chart in the guide for teachers shows the science and other curricular
areas a particular issue serves. The sciences identified are life science,
earth science, physical science, and science and society. The other curricular areas are language arts, math, social studies, and art. Among some of
the recent themes are "What Feet Do," "Making Things Move," "Changing
Colors," sea monsters of prehistoric times, and earthlings in space.

The 16 pages of every issue are colorful or are even fully colored, as
background white seldom shows. The layouts of the pages are appropriate
for the subjects and should captivate readers. Pages are full but by no
means crowded. Photographs and drawings of children are seemingly
placed whenever possible among the pictorial matter of the theme.

Although adult assistance with some of the text will be needed for children at one end of the intended grade range, no page is incomprehensible.

The *Blue* edition for upper grades continues the hands-on approach to science. Themes too are selected for the issues; however, the themes, do not parallel the monthly themes of the *Red* edition. This edition also is fully illustrated with photographs, drawings (informative and humorous ones), charts, tables, graphs, and maps on its 32 pages. Text and illustration continue to be about equally balanced, but the smaller typeface of the *Blue* edition allows for much more text.

In this edition's guide for teachers, skills and curricular areas are again charted; however, differences can be noted. In columns captioned "process skills," the following are checked off as appropriate: observe, use numbers, gather data, classify, predict and infer, hypothesize, experiment, and communicate. The curriculum areas accounted for, in addition to science, are technology and society, language arts, social studies, math, art, and health and safety. Among recent themes chosen are deep sea exploration, tornadoes and wind power, sun and light, physics of toys, and Antarctic adaptations. About five feature articles on the theme are listed in the table of contents. In issues examined, these too continue the double-page spread advantage by being two, four, or six pages in length. About five departments appear rather regularly under "News and Other Stuff."

Editions for teachers are available for both the *Red* and *Blue* student editions. The guides can be purchased separately at $19 each and are free with bulk orders. Each guide includes a copy of the student edition. Teachers who submit bulk orders receive a supplemental computer disc and 16 posters.   *Children's Magazine Guide*

Surprises

Children's Surprises, Inc.
P.O. Box 236, Chanhassen, MN 55317
Bimonthly; $12.95

The subtitle "Activities for Today's Kids & Parents" under the nameplate suggests the content of this bimonthly. Most of the activities require pencil or crayons, although a few ideas for things to do or make are presented along with some games to play. The magazine's intent is to furnish parents with the amusing cousins to workbook pages that will "build their children's educational skills." Most of the illustrations of the 40 some pages are line drawings; touches of color are added to many. Intended for ages 5 to 12, some of the 8¼-by-10¾-inch pages will be passed over by those children at either end of the range. Presently, cartoon characters and celebrities of family-oriented television shows appear on the covers. The magazine is highly pictorial, but the illustrations are undistinguished, sometimes even bothersome.

Many of the captions of the contents page continue to appear as they did in the first issues of 1985. "Word Wise" provides an exercise to familiarize children with some of the difficult words in the issue. In "Leading to Reading," phonics and verbs have been introduced to name some word play; one issue took a trip to the library. "Book Nook" offers reading suggestions. Matters mathematical are made playful in "Math Magic." "Amazing Animals," usually several pages in length, shares facts. Recipes are supplied under "Delicious Delights." Concern for others is stressed, in issues examined, in "I Am Special." "Kids' Corner" presents artwork and brief stories from subscribers, sometimes on themes announced in previous issues.

Other times and places are introduced in "Hooray for History" and "Around the World"; however, pages crowded with factual information, drawings, and exercises do not make for pleasant or interesting excursions. Inside the front cover are "Kids' Talk," letters to the magazine, and "P.S." (Palmer and Simenson), a letter to readers from the two editors, elementary school teachers who created the magazine. The kinds of exercises within an issue are plentiful: mazes and crossword puzzles, matching and identifying lessons, dot-to-dot and hidden pictures, and instructions to draw, color, cut, or fold.

Texas Historian
Texas State Historical Assn.
Richardson Hall, 2/306, University Station, Austin, TX 78712
5 issues a year: September, November, January, March, and May
$6

Intended for grades 6 to 12 and written by students in these grades, this magazine is a publication of the Junior Historians of Texas. Five or so articles from three to four pages in length are typically published in a 21-page issue. Biographical pieces are frequently featured, although there are also articles about buildings, places, and events. The writing is substantial, in thought and presentation. Bibliographies cite sources, including unpublished ones.

The five articles in one particular issue discuss the adventurous life of a young Belgian who was released by his seafaring kidnappers at Galveston (written by a fifth-generation descendant); a German immigrant of the 19th century; a president of a major university during the 1960s; a Houston philanthropist; and the little theater movement and the quarters set up in a Carnegie library. The writing is solid and readable. Some of the entries in its annual writing contests are published in the magazine. The submissions are judged "on the basis of organization, originality of the topic, writing style, documentation, and total interest of the paper." These high standards are reflected in many of the magazine's articles.

Black-and-white photographs, usually one or two to a page, accompany the articles. Typeface is legible although rather compact. Off-white paper of high quality is used for the 7-by-10-inch magazine. The cover is pictorial. No color is present; it is not necessary to the content. In most issues, the "Chapter Showcase" reports news of local chapters, state meetings, and other activities of the Junior Historians.

The magazine is published by the Texas State Historical Association in cooperation with the Center for Studies in Texas History at the University of Texas at Austin. The publication will be of particular import to one state, but, as with similar magazines, some of a state's history is either shared or of interest elsewhere. In this case, the nonfiction writing of young people is also noteworthy.

3-2-1 Contact
Children's Television Workshop
Edit: One Lincoln Plaza, New York, NY 10023
Subs: P.O. Box 53051, Boulder, CO 80322
Monthly; except February and August (10 issues)
$15.97

The sentence, "Children's Television Workshop explores the world," across the top of the cover announces the subject and publisher of this monthly for children 8 to 14. The full-color pages are packed with stories, puzzles, projects, experiments, questions, and answers about science, nature, and technology. The articles and activities are grouped on the contents page under "Features," "Departments," and "Square One TV." The cover photograph, always appealing and in color, frequently captures the drama of science.

The feature articles, typically divided into short paragraphs, are informative and picture (in addition to the science) people (especially children) in photographs or caricatures. Features in a recent issue suggest how to deal with a bully and detail how patents are obtained. An article about photographing a ladybug shows one shot of the hair on the ladybug's leg, 3,600 times life size. The four-page cover story about penguins of Antarctica links the cover photograph of Adelies with the centerfold pinup of Emperor penguins. In another issue, the feature articles tell in text and illustration about cats, facial expressions, Voyager 2, and an expedition to the North Pole.

Many of the regular departments turn up in about the same place from issue to issue and have some similarity from month to month, all of which introduce children to a trait of many magazines. Among the regular departments are "Factoids," amazing statistics and data often humorously illustrated; "Any Questions?", perplexing queries from subscribers regarding issues within the magazine's scope carefully answered in several paragraphs; and "Mail," letters from readers about previous issues. "TNT: Newsblasts" (formerly Tomorrow's News Today) reports brief items or stories about science-related subjects. "Slipped Disk Show" answers questions about computers, and "Basic Training" prints programs for home computers. Each month, a mysterious case challenges "The Bloodhound Gang," young detectives. "Contact Lens" highlights an animal, a volcano, or some other facet of the science world in a full-color photograph and includes a paragraph about the selected subject. "Reviews" covers books, games, and software. "Extra" offers miscellaneous puzzles, and "Did It" supplies the answers for the issue. "Square One TV" of the contents page often includes math-related puzzles, games, and tricks; however, some are not about math specifically. A three-page cartoon in one issue requires some calculations to make sense of the puzzlement presented.

Science is of interest to many children, and there is in the 40 some pages of this monthly much that is captivating, much that is curious. The layouts of the 8⅛-by-10¾-inch pages keep the reader's eyes, and presumably mind, jumping. The pages bearing fine full-color photographs are about equal in number to those with color drawings, the latter undoubtedly satisfying to children who like ludicrous illustrations.

Children's Magazine Guide

Trails see *Scholastic News: Trails*

Turtle Magazine for Preschool Kids
  Children's Better Health Institute
    Edit: Benjamin Franklin Literary & Medical Society, Inc., 1100
      Waterway Blvd., P.O. Box 567, Indianapolis, IN 46206
    Subs: P.O. Box 7133, Red Oak, IA 51591
    Monthly; except bimonthly January–August (8 issues)
    $11.95

The publisher attempts to combine entertaining reading with instruction, primarily about health. The table of contents is divided into two parts, "Health" and "More Fun." While in earlier years "More Fun" brought more health, the scope of the magazine has evolved to include material of a seasonal nature. Nutrition, safety, and good habits are promoted through stories, activities, and rhymes. At times, the content extends to other science topics. The magazine's title figure, Turtle, appears on the cover of each issue and, among other places, in his own three-page cartoon feature, "Turtle Tales." His silhouette is incorporated into the final letter of the magazine's nameplate, and it ends each article or story. Puzzles of many kinds separate the four-to-five-page stories, which, if not on the magazine's main subjects, are seasonal tales.

Intended for children two to five, the youngest range of the publisher's six periodicals, the magazine, as the others, centers on health. Regular departments include, in addition to the Turtle cartoon, "Our Own Pictures," reproducing art of subscribers, and "Ask Dr. Cory," parents' questions answered by the physician. A typical issue incorporates stories, rhymes, activities, and puzzles. Puzzles include mazes, hidden pictures, dot-to-dot challenges, matching games, and pages to be colored.

Simple illustrations in color and in black and white accompany the longer stories and rhymes. Animal characters populate a number of these pages and are depicted in fairly simple forms. Clarity of representation is enhanced when detail is limited to the hidden pictures. The short rebus stories and games are presented in black and white, and some are meant for coloring. The illustrations convey a sense of playfulness. Pastel colors are seemingly used more often than vivid ones and are a welcome contrast to the gaudy art of some magazines now entering the market. While the best of children's illustrations is not represented in the 48 pages, the artwork shows improvement over previous years when cartoon-like characters dominated.

Issues include humorous and light bedtime or naptime stories that can be read to the child. Although the publisher cautions free-lancers to avoid preachiness, some of the magazine's articles and verses are tinged with it. Games and crafts require some adult guidance. The youngest child targeted by this publication may have trouble, for example, with dot-to-dot puzzles that look simple but require sequencing of letters and numbers, skills that could be developed by using these games with an adult.

Much is here to occupy the hands and mind of the young child. Games and puzzles are intended to help children develop skills with words, numbers, and shapes and the operations performed with these symbols. Stories and poems are amusing. The highly pictorial 6½-by-9⅛-inch pages should be inviting to children who have not yet learned to read. A subscription would be a worthwhile investment, especially if the child already receives one of the fine nature magazines for the very young. Every issue, Turtle— of the full-color cover—gaily, even exuberantly, pursues a little adventure; most children would gladly join him and willingly follow the fellow through the content.

U.S. Express
Scholastic Inc.
Edit: 730 Broadway, New York, NY 10003
Subs: 2931 E. McCarty St., P.O. Box 3710, Jefferson City, MO
65102
Biweekly during school year (14 issues)
$13; $6.50 each for 10 or more subscriptions to same address

A new periodical from Scholastic, this one is intended for students of English as a second language in grades 6 to 12. The multicultural approach is refreshing and much needed in children's magazines. The emphasis on topics of more interest to young adults than children keeps this title from being entirely suitable for children below grade six. Full-color photographs on the 8-by-10⅞-inch covers introduce the major features. Issues tend to carry in their 16 pages a play, something about customs or religions, and descriptions of places in the United States. Regularly on the verso of the cover are the half-page "News and Views" and "Issue in the News." Questions at the end of each urge readers to give thought to the matters discussed. The back page, "Express Mail," usually pictures a person or group from a foreign country. The reader, by using the vocabulary list correctly, can find out something else about those pictured. A two-page photographic story in cartoon style regularly precedes the last page. Titled "American Pie," the setting of the dilemma is a pizza parlor; teenagers work out relationships that have cultural overtones.

Among the features, in issues examined, that need not be limited to the targeted audience are an adaptation of the play *The Diary of Anne Frank* and the playlet made of William Saroyan's "The Summer of the Beautiful White Horse." The colorful reports on Mardi Gras, marriage customs, and the American Indian Dance Theater might well be of interest to younger (English-speaking) children, and the vocabulary would be quite manageable. The layout of pages is attractive and varied. Drawings and photographs are well composed and reproduced. Full color is used on almost all pages.

The biweekly was created to help students adapt to their "new English-speaking environment." The content includes current events and issues of interest to teenagers, as well as history and geography. The edition for teachers spells out ways to use the student's issue, with its delineation of "vocabulary preview, words to teach, background, before reading, and discussion."

*U*S*Kids*
Field Publications
Edit: 245 Long Hill Rd., Middletown, CT 06457
Subs: P.O. Box 8957, Boulder, CO 80322
Monthly; bimonthly July/August (11 issues)
$18.95

"A Weekly Reader Magazine," this one is published for the home market. Many of the purposes of the publisher's classroom periodicals are adhered to in this 44-page monthly, but the format is quite different. The layout of the pages and the generous use of color, especially in photographs, imbue the magazine with liveliness. The interests of children are effectively addressed in true-life adventures and science features. The writing is clear, concise, and quite readable; the articles are brief in text. Intended for ages 5 to 10, the 8-by-10⅞-inch pages are highly pictorial. Color photographs and colorful upbeat drawings that accompany activities and puzzles fill most of the space available.

Although not readily evident from the contents pages, most issues contain four fully illustrated articles. Within the magazine, the articles are dubbed "real world" or "real kids"; often the publication contains two of each. The real-world articles frequently use members of the animal kingdom for their subject. The four-page lead stories in issues examined are about armadillos, sharks, and animal eyes. Each makes use of full-color close-up photographs, carries a few paragraphs of text, and concludes with a matching puzzle. The articles are written at reading levels appropriate to the intended audience; however, some puzzles raise questions of suitability. For example, the drawings of sharks accompanying the article are not sufficiently discrete for the young to make identifications, and the drawings on the page to which the reader is referred for help are even less distinctive. Two of four photographs of a field as viewed by bee, rabbit, hawk, and snake carry unexplained elements, and two others do not fit the descriptions in the text.

Other articles about the real world feature northern lights, mazes, and chocolate. The photographs and brief text of the astronomy article clearly and succinctly reveal the information a young child could absorb. The night shot of some mazes in a California park hints of adventure, although the mazes are barely discernible; a double-page spread that follows tests the reader's skill in negotiating a maze. In a colorful lively drawing, the process of changing cocoa beans into chocolate is shown; brief text helps clarify the steps. Quite appropriately, this feature ends with a no-bake cookie recipe. An advertisement announces that the magazine also brings articles about anatomy, robots, and current events, as well as stories about children who have made news in one way or another.

All in all, the pictorial articles about real kids in the issues examined have some qualities superior to the real-world articles. Each has clear color photographs of the profiled child, and each brings a story worthy of telling. Paragraphs about Miriam, daughter of a mixed marriage, are followed by a full-page family tree on which the child can record his or her own family. In another issue and article, David and his father, their tribe not specified, carve a totem pole; this article is followed by instructions to make a pole out of spools. A third issue's article relates how Atiya created the message and illustration for an antidrug T-shirt; true or false statements about drugs test the reader's knowledge of the subject. Another article tells about Courtney, a child with cerebral palsy who learned to ski. Each issue also usually contains a fiction story that is realistic or humorous; or a folktale; or a poem. Among some of the special games and projects found in issues examined are board games, magic tricks, and the making of a miniature book.

A really fine monthly feature is the centerfold. Mammal, reptile, bird, and small creature magnified have all been brilliantly captured in the exquisite full-color photographs. Back-to-back, two posters come in an issue. For each photograph, there is on a nearby page a rectangle bearing factual data and a miniature of the poster; children are encouraged to develop a 3 x 5 card file. Another regular feature is "Adventures of the Puzzle Squad," eight bounteous pages of puzzles, games, and activities meant to enhance reading, math, and thinking skills with pleasure. The squad is always made up of the same five children. The first page, a full-page drawing with hidden pictures, establishes a setting for the puzzles that follow. Among places chosen for these pages have been the Children's Museum in Boston, Plimoth Plantation, and Bemidji. On the other seven pages, in addition to a tongue twister or joke, can be found every conceivable form of word, picture, and number puzzle.

At the back of several issues has been running "The Pet Show," a full-page color photograph of a pet and a small photograph of the owner. (Children send in snapshots of their pets, and if selected, a professional photographer goes to the house to take the published photograph.) Also near the final pages is the regularly appearing "Kids Helping Kids," a citizenship feature in which a half dozen children offer suggestions about a problem another child has posed, such as handling emergencies when parents aren't home or fighting with siblings. Up front, to the right of the contents page, a puzzle related to the cover appears with consistency. The cover always pictures children in a full-color photograph. Smiles abound in issues examined.

The magazine mixes informative articles with puzzle pages. One often follows on another because a page to teach skills, albeit with humor, is usually related to the preceding article. Such a mixture is in keeping with the intent of the magazine. While at times the impression is that of a hodgepodge, the format is not inappropriate for this kind of children's magazine. (When the magazine first appeared, puzzles were by and large limited to the "Adventures of the Puzzle Squad" section.) The content should satisfy the intended age range, although with such an expanse, there will be sections of the magazine of lesser interest to any given reader. There is much to amuse in this relatively new magazine; however, in the words of an ad for teachers, "every part of the magazine has an educational purpose." *Children's Magazine Guide*

Walt Disney's DuckTales see *Disney's DuckTales Magazine*

Walt Disney's Mickey Mouse see *Mickey Mouse Magazine*

Wee Wisdom
  Unity School of Christianity
  Unity Village, MO 64065
  Monthly; except bimonthly June/July and August/September (10
    issues)
  $8

This periodical, first published in 1893, has a long and continuous history. The purpose of "A Children's Magazine from Unity" (its subtitle) is "character-building and its goal is to help children develop their full potential." The monthly is nonsectarian, even though from a religious publishing house. The upbeat tone does not necessarily align the title with a specific faith. The one obvious connection to Christianity is the regular printing of the "Prayer of Faith" and the "Prayer for Protection." The 48-page magazine is intended for children ages 5 to 12; however, the stories and activities are likely to be of most interest to children under 10.

The contents page is divided into two parts, "Stories and Poems" and "Things to Do." In the first section, a poem is sure to be listed, sometimes two. Usually five stories appear in an issue. Most of the stories are about a half dozen pages in length, although one is always much shorter. The editors try to adhere to a third-grade reading level. Familiar words of one and two syllables populate the pages. The work is apparently that of free-lancers, who are advised that character-building ideals should be emphasized without preaching and that language "should be universal, avoiding the 'Sunday School' image." The writing, while not particularly engaging, does enable young readers to cross the terrain without much difficulty. The intent is to "promote positive, happy thinking in the readers." Most stories have contemporary settings and main characters who are children. There is some anthropomorphism and, invariably, a happy ending. Children will probably find the tales amusing.

About 10 items are listed under "Things to Do." To the right of the contents page is regularly printed "Action Corner with Pete and Polly," one of several features that suggest ideas about caring and sharing. The centerfold opens to "What's the Good Word?", positive words (*love, joy,* and *gentle,* for example) with brief meanings presumably sent from "best boosters." Preceding the centerfold is news of the "Good Words Booster Club." Other regular pieces are "Writers' Guild," verses from children; "Dear Readers," letters from the editor; and "Dear *Wee Wisdom*," letters to the magazine. "Puzzlers" captions a few pages of hidden-object pictures, dot-to-dot drawings, word puzzles, and riddles. Other entries begin with "Let's" and lead to craft projects, gift ideas, and recipes, the last presented by a cooking goose. Instructions are clearly stated for all of these activities. The back cover allows the child to fill in words and complete pictures of a six-box story in which two children are happily engaged in a good deed.

The illustrations in an issue show slight variation in style. Some are soft and gentle, using pastels, and others, especially the line drawings, are more vigorous. Most likely, the illustrations are commissioned by the magazine because some illustrators are named frequently, and others seem to fit a mold. Full color is used on the covers and on a half dozen pages at the beginning and at the end of each issue. A touch of color is added to the middle pages to brighten the appearance. The layout of the 5½-by-8⅜-inch pages is not overcrowded; the typeface is dark and legible. The outside cover, which can be removed, makes a wall calendar for the month; the inside cover remains intact.

The subscription price continues to be one of the most reasonable for children's magazines. The monthly will find a warm reception in homes where the magazine's intent matches the parents'. In the words of the editor, the purpose is "to show children how to act positively by stressing the good." *Wee Wisdom* is available in braille, free to the blind, from Unity. *Children's Magazine Guide*

Weekly Reader

A graded series of four- and eight-page classroom newspapers with eight editions from preschool through grade six, *Weekly Reader* from Field Publications regularly brings to children news; current information about the community, the nation, and the world; and recreational reading, all designed to meet the interests and reading abilities of the average child at each grade level. Among the topics treated on the 8⅛-by-11⅜-inch newsprint pages are science, animals, government, entertainment, sports, people, and other children. Exercises in basic reading skills and comprehension are supplemented by word games, puzzles, mazes, and other activities. A guide for teachers, available for each issue, includes background information and further ideas, questions for discussion, and tests. The "Answer Key" in the guide will probably be helpful for the puzzles, but the exercises too might require a peek.

Weekly Reader Summer Edition appears as "A" for kindergartners and first graders and "B" for children in grades two to five. An eight-page issue is mailed to the home six times during the summer. The intent is to encourage children to continue reading and developing skills during the school holiday. Current events, science (especially nature studies), and true-life adventures are subjects of the articles, stories, activities, games, and puzzles. The price of an individual subscription is $3.

Weekly Reader Pre-K Edition
  Field Publications
  Edit: 245 Long Hill Rd., Middletown, CT 06457
  Subs: 4343 Equity Dr., Columbus, OH 43228
  Weekly during school year (24 issues)
  $7.20; $3.60 each for 5 or more subscriptions to same address
The lively and colorful front page of this four-page weekly Pre-K Edition regularly pictures Banana (a monkey) and his friends Frisky (a squirrel) and Jumper (a frog) in situations familiar to many three- and four-year-old subscribers. A four-color drawing fills most of the page; at the bottom, a paragraph provides instructions for the adult in calling the child's attention to the illustration and activity. In three recent issues, the anthropomorphic characters meet a mail carrier, play safely in the snow, and make a visit to the dentist's (female) office, where Jumper becomes hopelessly entangled in dental floss. Health and safety, among other topics, are treated on the front page.

The center two pages reflect the science and social studies of a child's world in black-and-white photographs and line drawings with a color tint. The fourth and last page is captioned "Fun for Us" and brings seemingly painless but fittingly challenging exercises to help the young note relationships of parts to the whole, classify objects, and coordinate eye and hand movements, to name a few. Page four of the 8⅛-by-11⅜-inch newsprint weekly, like page one, is in color. Page numbers, larger than usual, are in some issues boxed with the same number of geometric shapes so the child can learn both ordinal and cardinal numbers. Other opportunities for counting are also provided.

One of the two headings for the center pages is "All Around Us," words children might soon recognize by their frequent use. The features highlight people and events important to children. One issue introduces community helpers: a police officer, bus driver, and sanitation worker. Some issues have celebrated holidays; others have considered modes of transportation. Another issue explores the five senses through photographs (one for each sense) of happy playful children making use of their senses in pleasant circumstances. "Science for Us" is the other heading used in the center of the magazine. One feature pictures five animals (ostrich, snake, rabbit, dolphin, and kangaroo); under each photograph is a brief sentence describing how the animal moves, followed by a three-word question that asks "Can you leap?" or run and so forth. Special four-page supplements about topics in science and social studies are sometimes inserted.

On all pages are notes to the adult who is guiding the child through the subject matter. Suggestions pertain to ways to enhance language skills, skills of thinking and observing, and auditory and visual discrimination. A four-page guide for teachers accompanies bulk subscriptions. The leaflet would be of interest to parents who want to become involved in teaching their young the skills that prepare them for that great undertaking, learning to read. The guide identifies the purpose of each feature, offers ways to urge children to make stories from the pictures and to tell of their personal experiences, lists new or difficult words, and describes enrichment and follow-up activities.

With a subscription, the young child can receive an early introduction to classroom periodicals and some of their particular characteristics. Issues are delivered regularly, with a few exceptions pertaining to the school-year calendar.

Weekly Reader Edition K
Field Publications
Edit: 245 Long Hill Rd., Middletown, CT 06457
Subs: 4343 Equity Dr., Columbus, OH 43228
Weekly during school year (27 issues)
$4.50; $2.25 each for 10 or more subscriptions to same address

The first page of this four-page newsprint magazine frequently shows three animal characters joyfully involved in activities quite familiar to many kindergartners, the audience for Edition K. Zip the dog, Nip the cat, and B.J. the mouse have made front-page news in recent issues by celebrating a holiday and by playing together amicably. Some cover stories treat more serious subjects such as being approached by strangers and feeling ill. A sentence (or two) in large typeface and easy vocabulary is printed under the four-color drawing that fills most of the page. In fine print at the very bottom are notes to the teachers and parents who are helping the young with the initial page of the magazine. Activities are suggested that elicit stories from children about the illustrations and that require close inspection of the pictures.

The two center pages introduce the science and social studies of the kindergartner's world. "Our Science World" enters physics through such specific topics as magnets that serve functional purposes and explores the natural environment by showing the brown snowshoe hare of summer and the white fur of winter. Seasons and weather find their place in this section too. Under the caption "Our Big World," trips have been made to the veterinarian, a science museum, and the library. In another feature, Washington and Lincoln are profiled. In the notes for adults, understandings are specified and activities proposed. Four-page supplements to the center pages appear occasionally. One is titled "Let's Experiment" and deals with friction. Two pages of simple experiments are followed by a page of crayon rubbings with the challenge to children to make some of their own. In another supplement, a visit is made to a hospital. The back page, "Zip's Puzzle Page," features amusing activities that require kindergartners to put matters in sequence, to alphabetize, and to complete figures or pictures. Various skills are exercised, including learning how to follow directions.

The many brightly colored drawings and color photographs, along with a sprinkling of letters, words, and numbers, add up to a cheerful introduction to reading. Again and again, adults are urged to encourage children to talk about what they see in the illustrations. This too paves the road to reading. A guide for teachers, which could be used effectively by some parents, suggests ways to use and expand upon the various parts of each issue. Brief stories and poems are scattered among the instructions and ideas. Nip's citizenship letter, not in the children's edition, is meant to be read to children and to bring out comments about such values as honesty, fairness, and concern for others.

Weekly Reader Edition 1
   Field Publications
   Edit: 245 Long Hill Rd., Middletown, CT 06457
   Subs: 4343 Equity Dr., Columbus, OH 43228
   Weekly during school year (27 issues)
   $4.50; $2.25 each for 10 or more subscriptions to same address
Front-page news stories of Edition 1, a four-page weekly, are presented in color photographs with a few brief paragraphs of explanation. The remaining three pages carry half- and full-page items captioned "News Feature" when about matters of recent interest, especially those about people, places, and animals, and "Science News" when about the natural environment, health, or the physical sciences. "Good Citizen" Buddy Bear regularly brings a message as well as his puzzle page to first graders. Illustrations and titles of articles in large typeface dominate the pages; however, there is sufficient material to challenge those learning to read. Some illustrations are line drawings, but over half are often photographs, excepting the puzzle page. Full color is generally used on the front and back pages, with a single tint on the center pages.

The 8⅛-by-11⅜-inch newsprint periodical introduces news events and features to the young. Simple sentences explain or expand upon topics suggested by pictures. In one issue, the front-page headline, "Elephants in Danger?", is followed by a news feature on page two captioned "Good News about Eagles." The next page announces "All Teeth Need Care," a health item about brushing teeth. An elephant and eagle are among the objects hidden in the picture of the puzzle page. Stories in other issues cover icebreakers (ships) and icebergs; dinosaurs and fossils; and presidents, in honor of upcoming birthdays. Despite the brevity of articles, they are informative and written in a straightforward style. On "Buddy's Puzzle Page" can be found exercises that strengthen the understanding of initial consonants, blends and digraphs, rhyming, and sequencing, to name some of the language skills addressed. "Buddy Bear Good Citizen" is a weekly letter of several short sentences, the last frequently a question for children to consider. One letter pleads for saving the whales. Buddy's friend Nibbles the mouse often joins the bear in this feature.

Notes for adults explaining the text and offering suggestions for activities no longer appear, it seems, in the child's newspaper. The guide for teachers continues to give background information, as well as facts to share. Points to think about or discuss with children are mentioned.

Weekly Reader Edition 2
Field Publications
Edit: 245 Long Hill Rd., Middletown, CT 06457
Subs: 4343 Equity Dr., Columbus, OH 43228
Weekly during school year (27 issues)
$4.50; $2.25 each for 10 or more subscriptions to same address
Edition 2 of the weekly series, intended for second graders, gives front-page coverage to a recent news story that is pertinent to the young audience. A color photograph or drawing fills about two-thirds of the page; a few brief paragraphs written at an easy-reading level takes up the rest. Appearing rather consistently but not always at the same location on the two center pages are features labeled "News Corner," "Health News," and "Science News." These same pages bring the citizenship letter from Whiskers, while the last page offers "Squeaky's Skills Page." Color is used on the front and back pages, and a single tint brightens the center pages. Overall space is about equally allocated to pictures and text; photographs are frequently used.

From the evidence in three recent issues, it seems the editors are seeking to expand the circumference of the child's world. For this, there should be praise; such respect for the capabilities of the young is sometimes missing in magazines of other publishers. The headlines of the cover stories of two recent issues proclaim "Six Men to Cross Antarctica" and "New Organs Save Lives." The third addresses an environmental problem, "New Laws Stop Noise." Within this issue is a commemorative piece about Martin Luther King, Jr., which includes a fine photograph of him and two paragraphs about his contributions; the issue also contains an excellent description and diagram of the human ear, along with advice about protecting the ears from loud noises.

The articles that aren't specifically about current events take as their subjects aspects of the sciences and social studies. Topics cover a broad range and include the plant and animal kingdoms, health and safety, physical sciences, earth sciences, and people—at work, at play, and dealing with social concerns. This last topic also finds a niche in some of the citizenship letters. Usually, Whiskers the cat shares in his letter to girls and boys problems he has faced (for example, dealing with a boy who wants to cheat or damaging borrowed items) and asks readers what they would do. However, when it comes to accepting rides with strangers, the advice is direct.

The last page of each issue, "Squeaky's Skills Page," although Squeaky the mouse doesn't necessarily put in a personal appearance in each issue, carries out the language arts intent of the weekly. The top three quarters of the page bring three or four items, differing in any given issue. "Know the News" and "Words to Know" reinforce the vocabulary of the issue. "Think It Out" often requires another look at the contents. "Mystery Spot," in issues examined, poses questions that exercise map-reading skills. The bottom of the page holds the long-running cartoon strip, "Peanut and Jocko," the former an elephant, the other a monkey. The humor is in a play on words meant to tickle the young with a punchline tailored to their idea of fun.

Four-page supplements relevant to curriculum areas are frequently inserted. As in other weeklies of the publisher, the special guide for teachers could lend some aid to parents who want to help children gain further learnings from the issues. On the other hand, every issue of a newspaper need not be a teaching tool.

This newsmagazine makes a fine introduction to the newspaper-reading habit. The layout of the 8⅛-by-11⅜-inch newsprint pages is attractive and inviting. Sufficient space is allowed around words and pictures to ensure that the pages are uncluttered. Color photographs are clearly reproduced, often with the clarity of the best in daily newspapers for adults.

Weekly Reader Edition 3
Field Publications
Edit: 245 Long Hill Rd., Middletown, CT 06457
Subs: 4343 Equity Dr., Columbus, OH 43228
Weekly during school year (27 issues)
$5; $2.50 each for 10 or more subscriptions to same address

Third graders make up the target audience of Edition 3 of this classroom magazine of stories and photographs reporting news of interest to the young. Science and social studies blend with language arts to form the content of this four-page newsprint weekly. The cover story is followed by a page or more with the headings "News Short," "News Feature," "Health News," and "Safety News." Robbie Raccoon's citizenship letter is usually printed on page three, and the last page is captioned "Skills Workshop," a euphemism for reading comprehension exercises.

The cover page, often with a half-page color photograph and half a page of text, features such headlines as "Transplants Save Lives" and "New Law Helps Disabled People" and reports the activities of government officials and the findings of scientists. In the cover story, or on the center pages, might appear recent news about animals, health and safety, and natural phenomena and disasters, as well as current events at home and abroad. "Alaska's Wildlife and Oil," for example, introduces several controversies. Some attention is given to holiday celebrations such as the Chinese New Year festivities.

The anthropomorphic raccoon, in his regular column, shares the perplexities he faces as a member of the class that Mrs. Santos teaches. Relating to peers, completing assignments, and witnessing thievery are but some of the matters boys and girls are asked to ponder. In one issue, Robbie wanted to know of something special he could do for a friend in the hospital.

Two captions have appeared on the magazine's last page for a number of years; "Check the News" and "Your Vocabulary" test some of the learnings of the issue. "Think It Out," in issues examined, deals with parts of speech and "Mystery Spot," with map skills. The regular cartoon has a firm hold on the space at the page's bottom.

Four-page pullouts about curriculum areas are sometimes inserted in the weekly issues. A recent literature supplement of Paul Bunyan stories is undoubtedly more entertaining than the reading skills inventory, which only accomplished readers may relish. Other supplements feature topics in the social studies and sciences. One supplement visits Australia.

The cover photograph is generally in full color. The back-page cartoon is produced in more than one color. The center pages seemingly use only a single tint to brighten the layout. All the pages are attractive. The typeface is particularly legible, and text is carefully placed on the page. Neither words nor illustrations seem crowded.

The guide for teachers outlines ways to get the most out of an issue by identifying for many articles the purposes for teaching, by supplying background information and facts to share, and by suggesting ways to motivate reading and work on vocabulary development. Ideas are proposed to stimulate critical thinking and discussion. The answers to the questions of "Mystery Spot" are found in the guide.

Weekly Reader Edition 4
Field Publications
Edit: 245 Long Hill Rd., Middletown, CT 06457
Subs: 4343 Equity Dr., Columbus, OH 43228
Weekly during school year (27 issues)
$5; $2.50 each for 10 or more subscriptions to same address

With Edition 4 for fourth graders, the publisher shifts from the four-page weeklies of the primary grades to eight-page periodicals with cover stories about topics that also appear in adult newspapers. Recent front-page headlines report "Eastern Europeans Want Freedom" and "Blue Whales Are Endangered." Illustration and text continue to be about equally portioned in an issue, but a typeface smaller than that used in the magazines for younger children allows for more words on a page. Current events and the curriculum areas of science and social studies continue to provide content. Articles also discuss health and safety information and offer tips. Language skills are addressed in the exercises, and a vocabulary box is regularly placed on the front page. Most illustrations are photographs, many in color, and most are well selected and clearly reproduced. Photo credits are faithfully given.

The center pages generally carry a double-page feature. One about social studies lists "The Rights of the Child" according to the United Nations document. The cover story in this same issue is about the UN's efforts to help children. Other center features about geography focus on the Mississippi River and Central America. "Science News," in issues examined, introduces readers to micromachines, food labels, and medical advances. Items captioned "News Short" report on the civil rights monument in Montgomery, smoke detectors especially for children's rooms, and rescuing a baby kangaroo, to name a few.

Among the regular columns is "Citizenship," now free of the animal characters of the editions for younger children. An incident is related, and the reader is asked what to do. Options are suggested, and blanks allow for additional responses. The problem described is one that a fourth grader might well encounter in getting along with classmates and friends. "D.J.'s Space" (D.J. is a disc jockey macaw) brings jokes and puzzles, brief biographical pieces (and pictures) of sports figures or entertainers, and "Fantastic Facts." "Skills Club" rounds out an issue, frequently carrying sections titled "Recall the Facts" and "Your Vocabulary." Chart and map skills are also covered.

The articles are usually several paragraphs long and have one or more illustrations. The cover story often extends to the top half of the second page. The writing is straightforward, providing a good example of news reporting for the young. Although the vocabulary is controlled, there is no condescension in style. Touches of a color brighten the pages where full color is not used. A guide for teachers is available.

Weekly Reader Edition 5
   Field Publications
   Edit: 245 Long Hill Rd., Middletown, CT 06457
   Subs: 4343 Equity Dr., Columbus, OH 43228
   Weekly during school year (27 issues)
   $5.50; $2.75 each for 10 or more subscriptions to same address

The front page of Edition 5, for fifth graders, provides a pictorial view of the lead story, which is developed under "Main News" within. The center pages carry features about science and social studies, including history and geography. "News Shorts" appears in various places and covers a great variety of subjects. "Fun Break" usually falls on page seven, and the next (last) page deals with language skills. Color photographs are used on the cover and center pages. Elsewhere, black-and-white photographs are reproduced, along with drawings and other illustrations, including graphs and charts. To these pages a single color is often added for highlighting. Text has a slight edge over illustration in the amount of space allotted to it in the layout.

Recent cover stories examine U.S.–Soviet relations, the upcoming 1990s ("the decade of your teens"), and voluntarism. Among subjects receiving extended treatment on inside pages are endangered species and liver transplants, as well as safety and health topics. "News Shorts" ranges far and wide, covering dinosaurs, wrestling, child performers, young heroes, improvements for the handicapped, and breakthroughs in technology. All in all, the newsprint weekly does a fine job of alerting fifth graders to current events both national and international in scope without neglecting human interest stories. News of the sports and entertainment worlds is also reported.

"Fun Break" regularly brings jokes, seemingly submitted by youngsters across the country, and the Garfield cartoon by Jim Davis. "Fascinating Facts" and "Terrific Trivia" are sure to amuse. "Private Eye" shares a mini-mystery that can be solved by close attention to the facts and deductive reasoning. "Skills Page," a workbook sheet based on the issue's content, commands the reader to "Recall What You Read," "Listen and

Answer," "Build a Vocabulary," "Think It Out," and "Ask the Map." The tasks will not be so odious to good readers as the directives might suggest.

As with other editions, a guide is available to teachers for this 8⅛-by-11⅜-inch weekly.

Weekly Reader Senior Edition
Field Publications
Edit: 245 Long Hill Rd., Middletown, CT 06457
Subs: 4343 Equity Dr., Columbus, OH 43228
Weekly during school year (27 issues)
$5.50; $2.75 each for 10 or more subscriptions to same address

The Senior Edition, formerly *Senior Weekly Reader*, is intended for sixth graders and is the top of the ladder of *Weekly Reader* editions. The cover story of the eight-page newsprint weekly, as in the editions for younger children, remains highly pictorial but is developed in the centerfold pages under the caption "Main News." Headings that appear regularly for the briefer news reports include "News Update," "Science News," "Sports," and "News Shorts." The last pages carry "Fun & Stuff" and skills— decoding and comprehension lessons that will help children become readers of daily newspapers. Full color is used on the front page and center pages; others have a touch of color. Photographs are the illustrations most frequently used, but practically every issue also has drawings, some informative, some amusing. Charts, graphs, and maps are staples too.

Cover stories deal with topics of national and international significance. A recent front-page headline reads "Hole Grows in Ozone Shield." Others ask "Is Garbage Burying the U.S.?" and "Will Freedom for E. Germany Mean Trouble for U.S.?" The center section quite adequately outlines the issues and controversies surrounding the topics. Science news in these three same issues reports on the lake that erupted in Cameroon, running tests on jet crashes, and behavioral effects of television viewing on young children. The three brief reports on each of the general news pages of the three issues are of the curious type: viewpoints about when the tower of Pisa will lean too far, crossing the Soviet Union on bicycle, and the effects of cigarette smoke on dogs, to name some. Reports on sports range from a story about Joe Montana to one about disabled people on skis.

The citizenship lessons of the other editions have seemingly been replaced by columns about physical and emotional health by physicians and psychologists with expertise in child growth and development. Safety and health are also addressed in special articles. "Fun & Stuff" typically carries a half-page biographical piece about someone in the world of entertainment; "Senior Sleuths," a short mystery; and the Garfield cartoon of Jim Davis. "Skills Page" requires matching, completing sentences, filling in blanks, choosing correct answers, and deciding between true and false, to name a few of the exercises under such headings as "News Comprehension," "News Vocabulary," and "News Graph Reading."

A guide is available to teachers.

Welsh Publishing Group, Inc.
  Mickey Mouse Magazine ages 2–6
  The Real Ghostbusters Magazine ages 6–11
  Barbie ages 6–12
  ALF Magazine ages 8–12
  Disney's DuckTales Magazine ages 8–12
Entertainment magazines in tune with the mass media, the five quarterlies published by Welsh are young (with *Barbie*, dating from 1984, the oldest) and popular (all with circulations over 400,000). Highly pictorial and in full color, most content is portioned out in articles and departments a page or two in length, although each issue usually carries one longer piece. Except for *Mickey Mouse*, which has a section for parents, the magazines are 32 pages in length and 8 by 10⅞ inches in size. Capitalizing on "current passions" of children, the publisher attracts advertisers wanting to make connections. Thereby, illustrations are commissioned and printed that magazines with small circulations could not produce without making the subscription price exorbitant. The quarterlies will be on the market until interest in the title characters wanes, and then they'll go the way of *Muppet Magazine* and *Snoopy Magazine*.

The Winner
  Narcotics Education, Inc.
  12501 Old Columbia Pike, Silver Spring, MD 20904
  Monthly during school year: September–May (9 issues)
  $8.95; $5.95 each for 10 or more subscriptions to same address
Above each issue's nameplate is the line, "saying no to drugs and yes to life," which is the emphasis of every page in this classroom periodical from a nonprofit organization dedicated to education against drug use. Intended for grades four to six, the 16-page monthly carries short articles and several regular items. The publisher suggests that there is "a soft sale of the drug message," but some would say it is rather pointed. A touch of a single color is added to the 8⅛-by-10⅝-inch pages, although a different color is used for each issue. Simple line drawings are the chief graphic work, with silhouettes and photographs showing up now and then. On the cover, particularly bold strokes are used.

  The contents of issues and the layout of pages follow a rather consistent pattern. The first half of an issue brings three two-page articles, along with thought questions and activities for each. The center pages open to "Fun & Games," a double-page spread of word puzzles. These pages are followed by either "The Winner's Circle," a role model for the readers, or "Try This!", in which readers are urged to take on a project such as volunteering or starting a business. On the one-page "Winner's Mailbox," warnings from children in the form of drawings, rhymes, or dicta about "the dangers of smoking, drinking, and using other drugs" are presented. A regular column by a "Jr. Editor" furthers the message; a boy, probably at least in the highest grade targeted, serves as the editor in issues examined. The last two-page item is "The Winning

Team," a cartoon-like series about a group of seven children who take on such subjects as understanding peer pressure, being responsible, and getting along with others.

A guide for teachers (40-page booklet for a half year) is available that gives further information about the subjects of each student issue, along with activities and worksheets. A grid outlines the content for the year under the headings of specific drug knowledge, drugs and societal issues, and life skills and wellness.

World see *National Geographic World*

WOW!
Pilot Communications, Inc.
Edit: 25 W. 39th St., New York, NY 10018
Subs: 308 E. Hitt St., Mt. Morris, IL 61054
Monthly; $17.95

Primarily a magazine about young white male stars, this colorful monthly is intended for girls ages 8 to 18. Profiles and pinup photographs update fans on the latest activities and gossip of popular entertainers in the worlds of television, film, and video and audio recordings. The idols reigning supreme are likely to be seen in successive issues, even on the cover from month to month, and to be the subjects of the full-color centerfold posters and lengthier pieces. The 75-plus pages are chockful of pics and squibs about the fellows; however, all is in a lighter vein than similar magazines targeted for older teens.

The contents pages, two full pages of titles and come-ons in every issue, sort the fare into "Passionate Color Pinups," "Stories on Your Favorite Stars," and "Only in *WOW!*" The last heading includes some of the regular columns that announce contests, offer health and beauty hints, and answer questions from readers. In addition to letters to the editor, there are results of polls conducted by the magazine and drawings of celebrities submitted by readers. Each issue seems to print a monthly horoscope and to provide for pen pal connections. An analysis of the latter suggests that the average age of the readership is 13.

Writing!
Field Publications
Edit: Curriculum Innovations Group, 60 Revere Dr., Northbrook, IL 60062
Subs: 4343 Equity Dr., Columbus, OH 43228
Monthly during school year: September–May (9 issues)
$15.95; $5.95 each for 15 or more subscriptions to same address

A classroom periodical for grades 7 to 12, this monthly aims to motivate children to write. As suggested by its subtitle, "The Continuing Guide to Written Communication," the magazine's prime intent is not, however, to publish the work of the young; instead, it is to help them develop their writing skills through informative articles and exercises and with advice in features about well-known authors, living and dead.

Hardly a collection of workbook pages, the magazine offers sound suggestions and challenging thoughts to its audience. As with other periodicals from this firm, the publisher sets up major subjects that are addressed in each issue. Containing not as many subjects as their health magazines, this one carries three in addition to the cover focus: "The Power of Words," "Skills Review," and "The Writer's Craft." The contents pages also list "Writers at Work," conversations with published authors, among them Joan Aiken.

The focus articles in a year's subscription cover a great variety of forms of writing. In one year, for example, there is coverage of historical fiction, biography, poetry, book reviews, humor, ad copy, and publicity, as well as ideas about writing interviews and preparing opinion pieces. Other cover-page articles have discussed autobiography and research papers. The eight-or-so pages of these articles offer how-to instructions, examples, and goads that ought to make youths run for pencils or word processors. At the end of many features and articles is the directive "Write Now."

The shorter articles under the caption "The Power of Words" are meant to help students appreciate the vitality of the English language and to make optimal use of its potency. "Vivid Verbs Add Verve" suffices as an example. In "Skills Review," a regular columnist emphasizes the basics of grammar, usage, and punctuation and corrects common mistakes. Among the writers presented as models in "The Writer's Craft" are Charles Dickens, Washington Irving, O. Henry, Ernest Hemingway, and Gwendolyn Brooks. The few items that regularly appear at the bottom of the contents page include "Word Command," discussing the meaning and usage of selected words, and "Write In," with questions from students answered by guest authorities. Contributions from readers in "Student Writing" have included a page of cinquains and a two-page first-person account of an audition. In each issue, the readers are encouraged to try their hand at the forms presented. "Book Shelf" offers a lengthy review of a book of interest to teenagers.

The 7¾-by-10½-inch magazine printed on glossy paper is attractive and inviting. Photographs of writers and drawings that decorate provide all the illustration necessary. The arrangement of text on the 32 pages is varied, and consideration has obviously been given to breaking copy into easily managed pieces. The writing exhibits, quite appropriately, different but imitable styles. Authorship is noted at the article but not always on the contents page.

In some respects, this classroom magazine is a cross between the magazines for adults about getting published and language-arts textbooks. Happily, the more desirable characteristics of each are represented. Because there are many aspiring authors in junior high school, as well as upper elementary grades, the motivation to learn more about how to write already exists. There is no comparable magazine for this age level. Subscriptions for libraries and homes might well be considered, especially for children who do not have access to the magazine in their classrooms. Back issues remain valuable.

Young American
Young American Publishing Co., Inc.
P.O. Box 12409, Portland, OR 97212
Monthly; $9

Primarily distributed as a supplement to certain metropolitan and community newspapers, this 10⅜-by-13⅜-inch tabloid for ages 6 to 14 is also available to classrooms and individual subscribers. First published in 1983, the 20-page newsprint monthly became national in 1989. The masthead carries the line "America's Newspaper for Kids." Full color is used someplace on most pages, although half the pages of an issue bear advertisements. The emphasis is on "interests of today's kids," and the magazine provides coverage "from world news to rock stars and from science facts to sports." In editorial and advertising guidelines, it is stipulated that material promoting alcohol, tobacco, drugs, weapons, violence, and sexual behavior inappropriate for children will not be printed. The publication's intent is "to emphasize the positive aspects of life."

The front page, in issues examined, has a standard format. Featured headlines and their color photographs show children selected for their accomplishments: the youngest punk band; The Kids Comedy Club of a New York City school; and a 13-year-old Navajo whose work was displayed in an exhibit of paintings by children living on her reservation. In the left column under the caption "News Flash" are printed brief items of particular interest to children. Another brief story and full-color photographs run across the bottom of the front page.

Among regular items inside is "You and the News" on page three, with three or so items on the top and "At Issue" on the bottom, which asks five children (photographs included) such questions as "Should record albums be rated?" and "What would you like to change?" The page labeled "World" brings news from abroad; a color map and geographic data under "Where in the World?"; and five head shots of newsmakers, primarily adult and not necessarily from abroad, captioned "Do you know these faces?" A double-page spread in one issue focuses on "The First Americans"—articles about five tribes and a concluding piece on Indians today. Similar spreads in other issues are part of a continuing series about rivers, covering the Nile, Yangtze, and Mississippi. Other page headings include science, sports, and entertainment. "F.Y.I." brings assorted facts and reader contributions and questions. Puzzles, games, and "micro mysteries" round out the "For Fun" page. For beginning readers, a colorful page of word and picture puzzles is called "Upstarts."

A four-page curriculum guide, available to classroom teachers, provides further information about the subjects of some articles and suggestions for further activities, as well as a list of book and audiovisual resources.

Your Big Backyard
   National Wildlife Federation
   8925 Leesburg Pike, Vienna, VA 22184
   Monthly; $10

Preschool children ages three to five are targeted in this 20-page monthly. The wraparound of each issue is addressed to their parents. Splendid color photographs reign supreme in this magazine printed on high-quality glossy paper. Careful attention is given to clarity in the illustrations, including drawings. The magazine is intended to help young children "learn more about the world of nature and to appreciate the responsibility we all share in conserving it." Seemingly, there are more shots of the animal kingdom than the plant kingdom, but close-ups of either are spectacular. Consider the members of the animal kingdom presented in close-up in one issue: on the front cover, a young koala; a dormouse and her baby dormice; a kangaroo and pouch occupant; a hermit crab; a family of cheetahs, along with sketches of the animals on which they prey—gazelle, wildebeest, and hare; weasels in white and brown; a toucan; and on the back cover, an adult robin, insect clutched in mouth, tantalizing three wide-mouthed fledglings.

The full-color photographs, superb in composition and detail, invite comment and extended observation. The brief, simple text of sentences and questions, printed in a very large typeface, guides children to sharpen their viewing of the illustrations. Pictures of wildlife and natural objects are used to teach word recognition and number identification. Although preschoolers would not be expected to read all of the words, many of the readiness skills could be quite painlessly acquired. A two-page "Read to Me" story in each issue, as its caption suggests, is meant to be read to the young ones. On other pages, children are encouraged to make simple things in keeping with the subject of the magazine, such as an animal mask of a brown paper bag and a terrarium in a jar.

Puzzles and games are clearly presented; with minimal help from adults most children could complete them. In one issue, for example, a fanciful crosscut of a prairie dog's home challenges youngsters to identify six things that don't belong there (a potted plant, for one). On a double-page spread showing four different habitats, the child is to cross out the animal in each that doesn't belong and to color the animals that do. On another page, a whale emerges when certain spaces are colored blue, and on the opposite page, instructions are given for making a simple, silly animal puppet from a letter-sized sheet.

The three-page letter of the wraparound addressed to parents offers ideas and suggestions on how to use fully the content of an issue. The adult is fed the information that can be told to very young children, wordage that would clutter the pages of the magazine. The letter offers helpful and appropriate hints regarding ways to enrich and extend the monthly.

The issues are mailed to a subscriber on a three-year cycle. After the 36th issue, a subscription would return to the first issue. Supposedly, the youngster would be ready to move on to *Ranger Rick*. Libraries might have reason to handle the subscriptions differently. The name of a month appears on the cover of each issue. No year is given. Copyright dates with the publishing data give some hint of the publication date. A five-number code on the back cover indicates the cycle and month. Some issues with recent copyright dates show more revamping than others.

A truly fine magazine for the very young, *Your Big Backyard* succeeds in introducing preschoolers to the wonders of nature beyond that of their own backyard. The subject matter allows an approach to reading readiness far superior to the tiresome exercises of some other publications. The value of listening, viewing, and conversing in learning to read is not overlooked. But most of all, the color photographs are prime and of the highest quality. The visual exposure to nature for about a dollar a month continues to be a real bargain.

Zillions see *Penny Power*

Appendix A
Magazines of Religious Publishing Houses

While it might be supposed that churches and Sunday schools make known to parishioners magazine titles published for their denominations, they apparently have the same difficulty in finding out about these titles as other adults do in getting information about children's magazines intended for general distribution. Furthermore, several publishers classify their titles as nondenominational. This appendix, then, is meant to make available publishing data about magazines for children from religious publishing houses. Sixteen titles are listed below, including one available only in braille.

The main purpose of the list is to provide information about the availability of individual subscriptions. (Questions about bulk orders should be addressed to the publishers.) Parents and children wanting subscription information about a magazine of their church, about interdenominational magazines, or about magazines of a faith or denomination other than their own should find the list helpful. Churches (and their libraries) might want to enter subscriptions or make available sample issues of the nonsectarian magazines and those of other denominations and persuasions. School and public librarians should be able to answer some questions about religious magazines by using this appendix, even though these public libraries are not likely to enter subscriptions.

All the titles listed below are available through individual subscription. Each publisher has assured that a single subscription would be mailed directly to a home address. The titles are all magazines in the sense that there is variety in their content, both in text and illustration. Articles, stories, activities, puzzles, and games are included to various degrees. Although there is a range in quality (and certainly individual tastes will dictate preferences), each magazine meets the criterion of being acceptable, and none is poor in content or format. Many titles are not strongly sectarian, and some are nondenominational. Titles were not eliminated on the basis of sectarian bias, a prerogative of the publishers. In any number of the guidelines for writers, free-lancers were advised to avoid preachiness and to promote positive attitudes and perspectives.

All titles are intended for children through age 12, not 14 as in the body of this book. (The titles examined for 13- and 14-year-olds tended to move into subjects of interest to teens.) Titles targeted for boys only or for girls only are not included. Magazines fewer than 16 pages in length are not included, except for those that are issued weekly but mailed in monthly packets, so long as they total at least 16 pages in a month. (In the list below, this is noted as "Monthly in weekly parts.") Not included in the list are devotional booklets, Bible lesson sheets, curriculum support materials, newsletters, or newspapers. Titles available only through bulk orders are not listed.

By necessity, the list must be limited to publishers from whom responses were received. The net, however, was cast widely. Letters were sent to numerous religious publishing houses and were followed up by telephone inquiries. No attempt was made to represent various or certain religious bodies in the list or in the portion of titles on the list.

Although narrative descriptions of the titles would undoubtedly be useful, such annotations are beyond the scope of this book. Some information about the magazines can be gleaned from publication data and suggested age levels, along with knowing that all satisfy the criteria mentioned above. Within each entry, the name of the publisher follows the title. If the bent of the publisher is not evident in its name, it is specified in parentheses. The address given is for both the editorial office and subscriptions. When two addresses are provided, the first is for the editorial office and the second, for subscriptions. The frequency of publication is followed by the price for a single subscription. Age ranges are those suggested by the publishers. The number of pages in an issue and its size in inches are provided. The next line notes the year of first publication and a current circulation figure. Another annotation may follow.

Wee Wisdom is described in the body of this book because it is indexed in *Children's Magazine Guide*. See the description under its title.

Adventure
> **The Sunday School Board of the Southern Baptist Convention**
> 127 Ninth Ave., N., Nashville, TN 37234
> Monthly in weekly parts
> $9.50
> Ages 8–11
> 16 pp. weekly; 5⅜″ × 8⅛″
> 1962; 25,000
> (*More* is published for younger children.)

Brilliant Star
   National Spiritual Assembly of the Bahá'í of the U.S.
      Edit: 2512 Allegheny Dr., Chattanooga, TN 37421
      Subs: Bahá'í National Center, Wilmette, IL 60091
      Bimonthly
      $12
      Ages 5–12
      33 pp.; 8½″ × 11″
      1983; 2,500

Clubhouse
   Your Story Hour
   (Nondenominational)
   P.O. Box 15, Berrien Springs, MI 49103
      6 issues a year
      $5
      Ages 9–14
      32 pp.; 6″ × 9″
      1982; 11,000

Discoveries
   Beacon Hill Press of Kansas City
   (Church of the Nazarene)
   6401 The Paseo, Kansas City, MO 64131
      Monthly in weekly parts
      $6.50
      Ages 8–11
      8 pp. weekly; 5½″ × 8¼″
      1977; 52,000
      (Three titles are published for younger children.)

Discovery
   John Milton Society for the Blind
   (Nondenominational)
      475 Riverside Dr., New York, NY 10115
      Monthly; except July and August (10 issues)
      Free
      Ages 8–18
      1935; 2,000
      (Available in braille only)

The Friend
   The Church of Jesus Christ of Latter-Day Saints
      50 E. North Temple, Salt Lake City, UT 84150
      Monthly
      $8
      Ages 3–11
      48 pp.; 8¼″ × 10½″
      1971; 210,000

Guide Magazine
    Review & Herald Publishing Association
    (Seventh-Day Adventists)
        55 W. Oak Ridge Dr., Hagerstown, MD 21740
        Weekly
        $31.97
        Ages 10–14
        32 pp.; 5¼″ × 8¼″
        1953; 42,000

Happy Times
    Concordia Publishing House
    (Lutheran)
        3558 S. Jefferson Ave., St. Louis, MO 63118
        Monthly
        $6.50
        Ages 3–5
        16 pp.; 8″ × 8⅛″
        1964; 60,000
        (Also available in braille from Lutheran Library for the Blind)

Kids
    Moody Bible Institute
    (Nondenominational)
    Edit: 820 N. LaSalle Dr., Chicago, IL 60610
    Subs: P.O. Box 2062, Marion, OH 43306
        Monthly; except bimonthly December/January, April/May, and
        August/September (9 issues)
        $19.95
        Ages 8–13
        24 and 32 pp.; 8¼″ × 10¾″
        1988; 23,000

My Friend
    Daughters of St. Paul
    (Catholic)
        50 St. Paul's Ave., Boston, MA 02130
        Monthly; except July and August (10 issues)
        $8.50
        Ages 6–12
        32 pp.; 8⅛″ × 10⅞″
        1979; 6,200

Olomeinu/Our World
    Torah Umesorah; National Society for Hebrew Day Schools
        6101 Sixteenth Ave., New York, NY 11204
        Monthly during school year (8 issues)
        $8

Grades 3–8
16 pp.; 8½" × 10⅞"
1945; 16,500

On the Line
Mennonite Publishing House
616 Walnut Ave., Scottdale, PA 15683
Monthly in weekly parts
$12.80
Ages 10–14
8 pp. weekly; 7" × 10"
1876; 9,900
(*Story Friends* is published for younger children.)

Pockets
The Upper Room
(Nondenominational)
1908 Grand Ave., P.O. Box 189, Nashville, TN 37202
Monthly; except bimonthly January/February (11 issues)
$12.95
Ages 6–12
32 pp.; 7" × 9"
1981; 60,000

St. Paul's Family Magazine
St. Paul's Publishing Co., Inc.
(Catholic)
Edit: 14780 W. 159th St., Olathe, KS 66062
Subs: P.O. Box 772, Ft. Scott, KS 66701
Quarterly
$13.95
Ages 7–13
36 pp.; 8½" × 11"
1984; 1,800

Shofar
Senior Publications Ltd.
(Jewish)
Edit: 43 Northcote Dr., Melville, NY 11747
Subs: P.O. Box 852, Wheatley Heights, NY 11798
Monthly in October, November, February, and March;
bimonthly in December/January and April/May (6 issues)
$14.95
Ages 8–13
32 pp.; 8⅜" × 10⅞"
1984; 11,000

Young Judaean
Hadassah Zionist Youth Commission
50 W. 58th St., New York, NY 10019
Quarterly
$5
Ages 10–13
16 pp.; 8½″ × 10⅞″
1910; 3,812

Appendix B
Editions for Visually Impaired

Some of the magazines described in this book are available in editions for the visually impaired. The editions in braille and large print and on audio disc recordings are listed below. See the annotations in the body of this book for descriptions of the magazines.

The following magazines are produced by the National Library Service for the Blind and Physically Handicapped, Library of Congress. The titles are available through cooperating libraries at no charge to persons who are unable to read or handle conventional print matter because of visual or physical impairment.

> *Boys' Life*—braille
> *Children's Digest*—braille
> *Jack and Jill*—braille; disc, packaged with *Ranger Rick*
> *National Geographic World*—disc
> *Ranger Rick*—disc, packaged with *Jack and Jill*

Titles from Field Publications may be purchased in braille and large print. Inquiries should be addressed to American Printing House for the Blind, 1839 Frankfort Ave., Louisville, KY 40206. The titles currently available are listed below.

> *Weekly Reader Edition 2*   *Senior Weekly Reader* (large print only)
> *Weekly Reader Edition 3*   *Know Your World Extra*
> *Weekly Reader Edition 4*   *Current Events*
> *Weekly Reader Edition 5*   *Current Science*

Wee Wisdom is available in braille from its publisher, Unity School of Christianity. Braille subscriptions are sent free to the blind.

See also *Discovery* and *Happy Times* in Appendix A Magazines of Religious Publishing Houses.

Appendix C
Age and Grade Levels Suggested by Publishers

A magazine is listed only once in the two lists that follow. Both the lists, by age and grade levels, need to be checked when looking for titles appropriate for a child of a given age or grade. All ages and grades suggested are those indicated by the magazines' publishers. Magazines of publishers that did not furnish age or grade-level suggestions are not listed here.

Within the list by age, the magazines for youngest children are listed first. The magazines listed under each age are arranged from the shortest age span to the longest. Those magazines intended for children "under" certain ages are listed at the end of the age-level list. The list by grade level follows the same pattern.

The lists can be used for a certain age or grade level. It is necessary, however, to look at the specific age or grade level of interest and also the spans of the preceding ages or grade levels.

Age Levels Suggested by Publishers

1–12	*Plays*
2–5	*Turtle Magazine for Preschool Kids*
2–6	*Mickey Mouse Magazine*
2–6	*Sesame Street Magazine*
2–7	*Ladybug*
2–12	*Highlights for Children*
3–5	*Your Big Backyard*
3–9	*Chickadee*
3–12	*Mazputniņš*
3–12	*Rainbow*
4–6	*Humpty Dumpty's Magazine*

4–7	*Chuckles*
4–8	*Prehistoric Times*
5–10	*U*S*Kids*
5–12	*Surprises*
5–12	*Wee Wisdom*
6–8	*Children's Playmate Magazine*
6–10	*Hidden Pictures Magazine*
6–10	*Kid City*
6–11	*The Real Ghostbusters Magazine*
6–12	*Barbie*
6–12	*Cricket*
6–12	*Games Junior*
6–12	*Hopscotch*
6–12	*Ranger Rick*
6–14	*Prima Ballerina*
6–14	*Shoe Tree*
6–14	*Young American*
7–10	*Jack and Jill*
7–15	*Dolphin Log*
8–11	*Pack-o-Fun*
8–12	*ALF Magazine*
8–12	*Disney's DuckTales Magazine*
8–13	*National Geographic World*
8–13	*Sports Illustrated for Kids*
8–14	*Children's Album*
8–14	*Creative Kids*
8–14	*The Goldfinch*
8–14	*KidSports*
8–14	*Odyssey*
8–14	*Penny Power*
8–14	*3-2-1 Contact*
8–16	*WOW!*
8–18	*Boys' Life*
9–11	*Child Life*
9–12	*OWL*
9–15	*Calliope*
9–15	*Cobblestone*
9–15	*Faces*
10–14	*Free Spirit*
11–15	*Piano Explorer*

Preteen	*Children's Digest*
Under 14	*Skipping Stones*
Under 14	*Stone Soup*
Under 16	*Koala Club News*
Under 20	*School Mates*

**Grade Levels Suggested
by Publishers**

Pre-K *Weekly Reader Pre-K Edition*
K   *Scholastic Let's Find Out*
K   *Weekly Reader Edition K*
K–3   *Scienceland*
1   *Scholastic News: Pilot*
1   *Weekly Reader Edition 1*
1–3   *SuperScience Red Edition*
2   *Scholastic News: Ranger*
2   *Weekly Reader Edition 2*
3   *Scholastic News: Trails*
3   *Weekly Reader Edition 3*
3–7   *Daybreak Star*
4   *Scholastic News: Explorer*
4   *Weekly Reader Edition 4*
4–6   *Scholastic Sprint*
4–6   *SuperScience Blue Edition*
4–6   *The Winner*
4–7   *Current Health 1*
4–7   *Seedling Series: Short Story International*
5   *Scholastic News: Citizen*
5   *Weekly Reader Edition 5*
5–6   *Scholastic DynaMath*
6   *The Green Mountaineer*
6   *Scholastic Newstime*
6   *Weekly Reader Senior Edition*
6–8   *Junior Scholastic*
6–10   *Current Events*
6–10   *Current Science*
6–10   *Read*
6–12   *Career World*
6–12   *Illinois History*
6–12   *Know Your World Extra*
6–12   *Texas Historian*
6–12   *U.S. Express*
7–9   *Scholastic Action*
7–9   *Scholastic Math Magazine*
7–10   *Merlyn's Pen*
7–10   *Science World*
7–12   *Art & Man*
7–12   *Current Consumer & Lifestudies*
7–12   *Current Health 2*
7–12   *Scholastic Choices*
7–12   *Writing!*

Appendix D
Year of First
Publication

The year of first publication, the year in which a magazine was founded, is given in the following chronological list for the magazines of publishers that supplied this information.

1893	*Wee Wisdom*
1902	*Current Events*
1911	*Boys' Life*
1922	*Child Life*
1927	*Current Science*
1928	*Weekly Reader Edition 3*
	Weekly Reader Edition 4
	Weekly Reader Edition 5
1929	*Children's Playmate Magazine*
1934	*Weekly Reader Edition 1*
	Weekly Reader Edition 2
1937	*Junior Scholastic*
1938	*Jack and Jill*
1940	*Texas Historian*
1941	*Plays*
1946	*Highlights for Children*
1947	*Illinois History*
	Weekly Reader Senior Edition
1950	*Children's Digest*
1951	*Pack-o-Fun*
	Read
1952	*Humpty Dumpty's Magazine*
	Scholastic Newstime

1954   *Rainbow*
1957   *The Winner*
1958   *Weekly Reader Edition K*
1959   *Mazputniņš*
1960   *Scholastic News: Explorer*
        Scholastic News: Pilot
        Scholastic News: Ranger
        Scholastic News: Trails
1966   *Scholastic Let's Find Out*
1967   *Know Your World Extra*
        Ranger Rick
1970   *Art & Man*
1971   *Sesame Street Magazine*
1972   *Career World*
1973   *Cricket*
        Stone Soup
1974   *Current Health 2*
        Kid City
        Koala Club News
1975   *Current Health 1*
        The Goldfinch
        National Geographic World
        Scholastic Sprint
1976   *Current Consumer & Lifestudies*
        OWL
1977   *Daybreak Star*
        Scholastic Action
        Scienceland
1978   *Writing!*
1979   *Chickadee*
        Cobblestone
        Odyssey
        3-2-1 Contact
        Turtle Magazine for Preschool Kids
        Your Big Backyard
1980   *Creative Kids*
        Penny Power
        Scholastic Math Magazine
        Weekly Reader Pre-K Edition
1981   *Calliope*
        Dolphin Log
        The Green Mountaineer
        Reflections
        Seedling Series: Short Story International
1982   *Scholastic DynaMath*
1983   *Misha*
        Young American
1984   *Barbie*

Faces
Surprises
1985   *Merlyn's Pen*
Shoe Tree
1986   *WOW!*
1987   *Children's Album*
Free Spirit
Prehistoric Times
School Mates
U*S*Kids
1988   *Chuckles*
Disney's DuckTales Magazine
Games Junior
Mickey Mouse Magazine
Skipping Stones
1989   *ALF Magazine*
Hidden Pictures Magazine
Hopscotch
KidSports
Prima Ballerina
The Real Ghostbusters Magazine
Sports Illustrated for Kids
SuperScience
1990   *Ladybug*

Appendix E
Circulation Figures

The circulation figures in the list below are those sent by the publishers. Some publishers reported press runs and others, paid subscriptions. Figures representing readership totals, including "pass-along" readers, were not asked for, and it is hoped such figures are not given in the numbers below. The magazines that failed to provide data or usable information are not listed here.

4,800,000	*Young American*
2,800,000	*Highlights for Children*
1,712,290	*Weekly Reader Edition 1*
1,700,357	*Weekly Reader Edition 2*
1,485,140	*Weekly Reader Edition 3*
1,473,780	*Sesame Street Magazine*
1,400,000	*Boys' Life*
1,379,317	*Weekly Reader Edition K*
1,300,000	*National Geographic World*
1,279,376	*Weekly Reader Edition 4*
900,000	*Ranger Rick*
859,260	*Weekly Reader Edition 5*
700,000	*Mickey Mouse Magazine*
600,000	*Sports Illustrated for Kids*
580,000	*Your Big Backyard*
577,706	*Scholastic Let's Find Out*
551,670	*Science World*
543,460	*Weekly Reader Senior Edition*
500,000	*Barbie*
480,000	*Turtle Magazine for Preschool Kids*

469,397	*Weekly Reader Pre-K Edition*
442,026	*3-2-1 Contact*
426,391	*Current Science*
405,075	*Read*
400,000	*ALF Magazine*
400,000	*Disney's DuckTales Magazine*
400,000	*The Real Ghostbusters Magazine*
320,000	*Jack and Jill*
309,358	*Kid City*
250,000	*Games Junior*
240,000	*Humpty Dumpty's Magazine*
237,067	*Current Events*
233,000	*U*S*Kids*
200,174	*Know Your World Extra*
177,000	*Current Health 2*
160,000	*Wee Wisdom*
150,000	*Penny Power*
138,843	*WOW!*
130,000	*Chickadee*
130,000	*Cricket*
130,000	*OWL*
123,056	*Bonjour*
120,000	*Children's Playmate Magazine*
110,000	*Children's Digest*
100,000	*Surprises*
96,000	*Dolphin Log*
92,151	*Odyssey*
87,000	*Current Health 1*
82,000	*Writing!*
80,000	*Career World*
75,000	*Child Life*
65,000	*Koala Club News*
61,216	*Piano Explorer*
48,000	*Current Consumer & Lifestudies*
47,000	*Cobblestone*
35,000	*Pack-o-Fun*
35,000	*Prehistoric Times*
30,000	*Chuckles*
28,000	*Plays*
25,000	*Children's Album*
25,000	*The Winner*
16,000	*Scienceland*
12,000	*Faces*
11,000	*Creative Kids*
11,000	*Stone Soup*
7,000	*Illinois History*
5,000	*Calliope*
4,538	*School Mates*

3,500	*The Green Mountaineer*
3,200	*The Goldfinch*
3,000	*Hopscotch*
2,500	*Skipping Stones*
2,000	*Free Spirit*
1,500	*Texas Historian*
1,000	*Rainbow*
1,000	*Shoe Tree*
800	*Reflections*
600	*Mazputniņš*

Subject Index

Each title described in the body of this book is placed under one subject heading.

Selma K. Richardson is a professor at the graduate school of Library and Information Science at the University of Illinois at Urbana-Champaign, and the author of *Magazines for Young Adults* (ALA, 1984). An active member of the American Library Association, Richardson has served on various committees, including the Newbery and Caldecott award committees for the Association for Library Service to Children, a division of ALA. She received her doctorate from the University of Michigan, where she is a distinguished alumnus of the School of Library Science.